The Li

MW00881496

Short Sayings and Prayers

Selected from the rare works of Thomas A Kempis
1836

St Athanasius Press
All Rights Reserved 2014

ISBN-13: 978-1497561847

ISBN-10: 1497561841

St Athanasius Press
133 Slazing Rd
Potosi, WI 53820
melwaller@gmail.com
(email is the best way to reach us)
www.stathanasiuspress.com

Specializing in Reprinting
Catholic Classics

Check out our other Titles
at the end of the book!

CONTENTS

Preface

The complete works of the "reverend and pious" Thomas A Kempis are exceedingly rare in this country and written in a language inaccessible to the majority of readers. Few only of his writings have been translated. The largest treatise, the "Imitation of Christ," ascribed to him is familiarly known to all the Christian community. The publication of 40 editions of this in the original and 60 translations of it into other languages, fully attest the regard with which it is perused. It has been instrumental in ripening more fruit for the kingdom of heaven than perhaps any other human effort. God in His providence has condescended to manifest singular favor towards it and now, after the lapse of more than 350 years, no treatise, on practical religion is more universally beloved and esteemed by persons of devout spiritual tastes.

It would naturally be expected that any other breathings of so holy a man might possess the same sweetness and devotional feeling. Although this expectation is certainly realized, I am not aware, with the exception of two tracts, the "Valley of Lilies," and the "Soliloquy of the Soul," that any other of his writing have been translated. These two with copious extracts from other pieces, may perhaps be given to the public at a future period, but the intimate connection of most of the remainder with monastic duties and Catholic ceremonies might interfere with their favorable reception.

The present little volume is a collection of the "pithy sayings" of Kempis, compiled from all his works, excluding the "Imitation," by Gerhard Tersteegen, an evangelical pastor of a church in a village in Germany. It was neither his design nor expectation, to extract all the similar interesting passages. Yet he has quoted enough "to strengthen and to nourish many a hungry soul, with the substance of all knowl-edge.". Some of his prefatory remarks will be read with pleasure by all admirers of Christian ardor and simplicity.

2014 Update:

A number of Kempis writings have been translated into English since this book was published in 1836. St Athanasius Press is working to bring all of Thom-as A Kempis' works back into print. Some of those that have been reprinted include: Vera Sapentia or True Wisdom, A Thought From Thomas A Kempis for Each Day of the Year, Collection of Thomas A Kempis Classics, A Golden Book of the Three Tab-ernacles and more will soon follow. Please check out our titles at the end of this book or our website: www.stathanasiuspress.com

The Little Kempis or
Short Sayings and Prayers

IN ANGULO CUM LIBELLA. I have everywhere sought after tranquillity, but have never found it, except in corners and with books. Kempis

1. It is indeed good to me to attach myself to God. O short and sweet word! By which one gains God and shuts out the world. What farther ought one to say or what farther can one desire? Is it not enough?

2. Thou must no desire to be running here and there, but thou must be solitary, the solitary mingle in no fellowship with externals.

3. Let thy conversation be only to the One and when He goes away, sit solitary and bear all patiently.

4. Temptation is a fire which proves the pure gold and burns up the dross. See thou, O man, what thou art? The heavenly refiner melts and the children of Levi purify.

5. All is not gold which glistens, nor is all chaff or counterfeit that comes under the flail, or is in the fire. God looks upon the heart and the intention.

6. The whole of this present life is, but one short

night. My days are short and evil and are soon to end. They are to be as though they had not been.

7. O that the world was all withered in my heart and the master my God, the immortal bridegroom was alone lovely to me.

8. That pleasure which flows with the current of this life is indeed a deceitful bitter cup. One may drink thereof when he desires. He will nevertheless after all be compelled to pay dear.

9. Fly from me, thou deceitful fondness for the world and all foolish pleasures of the flesh. Thou distractest and deceivest many, but in the end thou quitest and drownest them. Alas, for those who trust in thee! Alas for those who are drowned in thee. But come here and approach me, O holy contempt and perfect corn of all the pomp of this world and thou salutary recollection of my pilgrimage, never depart from me.

10. Whoever is dead to the world, who is not in the world, but in God, loves Him, so likewise is he who thinks and speaks thus and who looks upon the things without as though they were not.

Ejaculation

O my God! Thou art my only possession - alone

pleasant and sweet - to talk of Thee is sweet to those that love Thee - to think of Thee is lovely to the devout whose heart is not in the world, but is hid with Thee in heaven.

11. Sensuality covets those things that are without; desires amusement, looks on present and neglects future things. She avoids whenever she can things bitter and hard, that so often are salutary to the soul. She does not allow the soul to remain in silence or tranquility, but crowds it with various fancies which one can scarcely tell, but in truth are nothing worth esteem.

12. It is useful to seal and close up the heart, lest haply that Beloved withdraw and flee away, whom a pure and lowly heart especially seeks and searches after.

13. A God loving soul wishes and prays that God may make Himself know to all men and convert and draw all to Himself, that thus He may be praised and glorified of all.

14. O how profitable, how delightful and charming is it to sit in solitude and be quiet, talking with God and partaking alone of the highest blessing in which all good consists! O that I also may be united to this simple holy good, that I may be seduced by no inclinations or diversion to perishable things.

15. Wander not abroad, my soul, after the vanities and follies of the world, but turn thyself to thy master, thy God, who is Himself the source of all consolation.

16. It is all vain which we obtain by begging from a poor man. There are the rich who can grant us enough of all we desire. So all creatures are poor to comfort us, but God. He is rich in grace and gives to each one kindly and never upbraids.

17. Look again, soul, look again to Christ in retirement of heart. It is not safe long to remain without. Refuse to place your confidence without, when you would obtain satisfaction within.

18. The soul that rambles much round about is subject to many plots, but the quick returning (to the Ark) little dove, enjoys protection.

19. A holy soul whose conscience is pure towards God and is adhering to no vanities, yet becomes corrupted by the love of only one "thing".

20. A holy soul is one which relies in no way on any creature, but fastens all its hopes on God.

Ejaculation

My God, how happy is that heart which burns with

love to Thee! How much joy has he whom no vanity of the creature diverts. Is it not of such an one, he also sings in the Psalms, whom have I in heaven, but Thee and what on earth do I desire besides Thee?

21. Blessed is the soul that throws away external and temporal repose and all that appertains to comfort of the flesh and gladly for the sake of Christ assumes trouble and want.

22. Blessed is the soul that commits itself to God, to do with it as shall please Him.

23. Bless is the soul that never seeks its own glory, that never desires to do its own will, but designs, loves and proposes in all things the glory and will of God.

24. Blessed is the soul that alienates itself from all temporal objects and preserves itself pure before God in everything.

25. Christ says: I am thine only and chosen beloved. I am thy exceeding great reward, but be humble when things prosper and firm when they are adverse

26. O, that I might enjoy the sweetness of a holy soul by which the sense asleep it is led up in the spirit and is elevated above itself in the arms of its beloved and united with God in the bond of in-

ward love.

27. The soul has peace that loves Christ sincerely and the eyes of whose heart though turned off from Him, always inquires from Him what is well pleasing to Him. Then it walks peaceful and regular and in its joy no stranger has part.

28. He is One and there in none like Him. He is my God and all things are nothing to be compared with Him. He is my most fervently beloved and the truest friend whoso thus loves Him. He never more forsakes for He associates Himself gladly to the loving. And when now and then He hides Himself or permits us to be afflicted, He does it not to abandon such an one, but to prove him to purify and teach him.

29. Jesus says: See here am I, say, what is it to thee to die anew? Art thou already forgetful that thou must endure and labor for me.

30. O how noble thou art, soul, what a wondrous power is concealed in thee. Thou canst not rest if thou hast not obtained the highest good and considered thy last end.

Ejaculation

My God, what joy can I have in the world when

I consider the uncertainty and frailty of all things below heaven. But of Thee I am sure that Thou art good and that Thy Mercy endureth forever to all who trust in Thee.

31. Out of one is many, not out of many one. Watch to seek much, untie yourself to one, adhere to one, for in one all exists.

32. Men may seek numerous and different things from without, but see thou alone that internal happiness then art thou enough.

33. He who seeks now this and then that seeks little after that pure and simple one and concerning that one, hence he finds no lasting peace.

34. What concern all things to thee, my soul, who ar seeking another? Truly, nothing. I abhor all these for one is my good, one I love, one I seek and this one is to me better than all other good.

35. What prevents, my soul, that thou shouldst not leave all for the sake of Christ?

36. Thou mayest turn thyself whither thou wilt, always wilt thou find trouble and vexation if thou turn not to thy Creator for He is thy peace and sure rest.

37. O sweet companionship with Jesus and under

he wing of Jesus~ O, welcome union, full love and loveliness of the Holy Spirit. How much better felt than I can express! This is necessary for the soul which has made itself a stranger to all the world.

8. Jesus says: If thou art willing and hearkenest to Me, then thou shalt see every good. When you do what I say, then shall you be My friend. When you shall choose Me and love Me above all, then shall happen to you of my Father all which you wish.

9. He who wishes, follows and seeks the one he loves and serves him. What concerns me here? I am certain that Jesus is the man of my soul and for His sake I would not forget to languish and die if duly I might ever share in His love. To Him; therefore, will I attach myself for He pleases me and I can find no better friend.

0. O how much should I love and reverence Him through whose merit and grace I have been sought and redeemed? Therefore I ought to be to this beloved as an only son to his mother.

Ejaculation

I cannot say, I have enough. No present possessions please, but Thou Lord my God art the good that I wait for and in which I trust.

41. My beloved works in me with change. I feel not always what disquiets me and I enjoy not always what I admire, but there comes evening and there comes morning and also (full) day.

42. Jesus says: I am the ever present and most heavenly. I am the most true and from soul the farthest removed.

43. Jesus says: A moment I leave the loving soul that I may learn if it loves sincerely. To love sincerely, he has said is not to love Me for the sake of thyself, nor for the temporal advantage, nor for spiritual consolation, but to love Me for the sake of Myself

44. Shame to thee that thou always continuest weak and tender, learn to eat strong food and not children's milk. Appear for once under the strong third David. Take thy cross upon thee and follow me.

45. Jesus says: I like not to see thee yield so soon and lose thy hope. Seest thou not Me, yet art thou seen by Me, to whom justly thou shouldst confide thyself and all things.

46. Thou art deceived by thy self love and whilst thou forgettest the giver, thou misusest the gift. I have made thee intoxicated, but thou hast forgotten that the grapes were from my vine. Now this teache thee what thou art, and how much strength thou has

Is it because from thyself thou hast received it that thou hast not been able to retain it? But hast thou not been able to retain it? I understand that thou hast received it from above? Consider how necessary I am to thee, how sufficient and alone mighty am I to fortify thee in all good! Why is it well with thee without me?

47. Jesus says: What has thou of thyself done wrong in passing over to strange lovers? What has appeared displeasing in Me?

48. Jesus says: turn to me, it is enough that thou has hitherto run round about.

49. Jesus says: I leave thee a little while that thou mayest see My presence is most supremely necessary, not only in one or in the greatest things, but indeed, in all business, in all places, at all times, early and late, wherever you are, at home or abroad.

50. Jesus says: I give thee liberty to return to Me as often as thou feelest that I am necessary to thee. I have not shut My bowels of compassion to those who cordially and earnestly desire Me.

Ejaculation

O that I had something, my Lord, that I might give to Thee and that was acceptable in Thine eyes. What wilt Thou have, dearest Lord, who needest not of my possessions, I will, Thou sayest, have all, give Me thyself, then hast thou given Me all. O Jesus, fountain of all good, source of life, source of grace, source of sweetness, source of eternal knowledge, bestow on me the gift of Thy heavenly spirit, teach me always to give thanks and to give up myself for all things, this is the most acceptable service I can render to Thee. This I feel, to this I agree. Understand, see, I am wholly Thine, all that I have is Thine.

51. Jesus says: Thou hast not chosen Me, but I have chosen thee, my compassion has been extended towards thee. Dare anyone now to murmur against thee because thou hast approached Me. Indeed, this complaint is not against thee, but evidently against Me, Me who receive sinners and eat with them. And why shouldst thou not exercise thyself in My kindness?

52. Jesus says: I have no need thou shouldst offer me anything. I desire only thou should love me out of a pure heart, that is enough. Whereupon I answer. Shame! That in me there is nothing whereby I can attest my love to Thee. He again shall say, I expect nothing like that, they love is of itself enough, let that only be ardent and abide in Me.

53. Jesus says: I am so bountiful and loving that

I am always willing to bestow more than thou to repent, more willing to give than thou to ask of me. What affrightens thee then? Why art thou so fearful to approach one of great kindness? And why desirest thou to withdraw from my grace, who art so affectionately bidden?

54. Wilt thou wait to become worthy before thou approach hither? When wilt thou become worthy of thyself? When only the pious and the worthy the great and perfect man dare to come, to whom shall publicans and sinners go? Therefore come to Me, thou unworthy, so mayst thou become worthy and thou wicked, so mayst thou become good.

55. How can the confiding soul so render itself lovely and acceptable as to engage his heart in pious contemplations before God, on His beloved? That thus, because she cannot yet discern Him with a clear and sanctifying perception, she may at least by incessant recollection make Him to be as it were present.

56. O that the flesh the countenance of the heart, may never grow cold in seeking, but ever become more ardent from day to day.

57. Stand not still my soul, for this is not thy rest, but raise thyself upwards and ascend to Him, who has created thee.

58. Through Jesus and in Jesus thou mayst find abundance which can sustain thee in all anxiety. The more eager thou approachest, the sweeter and more condescending will be come nigh thee.

59. A devout soul sheds tears of love, but in consideration of perishable things, it subjects itself to the holy tribunal and gives thanks.

60. I know in whom I have believed, and I am sure, that it is easier to deny that heaven and earth exist, than to deny there is a God. And I know that God himself is the good of my soul, and that I never can be blessed without his perfect contemplation.

EJACULATION. Dear Lord! Pour out on me Thy greater grace in this life, or take me soon out of this world, that my separation from Thee be not serious: to live long, and that life not a better one, is to accumulate punishment.

61. Where is my God? Whom to have once seen is to have learnt all.

62. Jesus is thine only and especial beloved, who feeds among the lilies and longs to repose between thy breasts. Who has shown thee so much kindness as He? Who has loved thee with greater love than He?

53. Come to Jesus, give thyself to Him, open thine heart to Him, and tell for once before Him what thou hast so long borne concealed.

54. Thou mayst be in affliction or joy have always thy refuge in Jesus. On His account, thou must willingly despise all amusements, and on His account all bitter and loathsome things, be tolerable, and for His sake, be pleased wherever thou goest.

55. Despise all things in the world as dirt and poison.

56. The frequent visits of relations cause disquietude of heart. The world passes away with its lusts, thou doest also, and thy relations with thee.

57. Thou canst not love God perfectly, if thou dost not despise the world and thyself for the sake of God.

58. O brother pilgrim, where are they companions with whom thou formerly hast laughed and sported? I know not, they are taken away and have left me. Where is that thou sawest yesterday? It is vanished. Where is that thou Hast luxuriantly eat and drank? is all there. What injures thee, now that thou hast restrained thyself? Indeed nothing. Therefore he is wise, who serves God, and despises the world with sensual enjoyments.

69. Ah, seldom is one found here who seeks God purely, subdues himself perfectly, and forsakes gross enjoyments.

70. He who restrains himself from permitted things, is the better able to restrain from forbidden things.

EJACULATION. I will sacrifice myself entirely to Thee, and command Thy mercy for me forever. Lord, my God, all my actions stand through Thy compassion, and all peculiar reward is nothing, if Thy immeasurable good and compassion is not thereby; and this is my expectation and my trust.

71. The testimony of conscience is a cause of purity, an overseer of peace, a chamber of devotion.

72. He who maintains purity of mind and life, is as an angel; he who agrees to crime, and inclines himself to sinful thoughts is a servant of the devil.

73. Love is overcome by love. When the love of God enters, all transitory enjoyments give way in the heart.

74. All is nought; king, pope, letters patent. The end of all is death, corruption, ashes. One may elevate himself as high as he wishes; it is nothing, death takes them all away. Blessed is the pilgrim who has a habitation in heaven.

75. Perfect virtue is not attained suddenly, but gradually with many sighs and pains, with a fast purpose to overcome when one puts on such manifold power, namely, when he restrains himself, often the endurance of evil.

76. Blessed is he who extracts good from everything, and out of affliction makes gain. He who loves God, accepts the bitter and sweet, as alike from Him, and thanks God.

78. He stands well and sure, who places his trust not in himself, not in men, but in God.

79. The silence of the lips is a great aid to attain peace of heart.

80. He who desires to please God, to establish his heart and lips, will never lose the grace of piety, nor disturb the peace of the Beloved.

EJACULATION. How much have I sinned in this that I have not yielded and given up all to Thee. For am made to love Thee, and to enjoy Thee. I only am following the creature, but in it have found no peace of mind. Turn me, Lord, again to Thee, and leave me not to mind earthly things.

1. It is good for me to hold fast by God. Thou knowest that I am not weary of Thee. O, give ear to

me and hear me.

82. One is never so guileless or devotional, as when pains or disease befall him. Thus when thou art in afflictions, and calamity of heart, thou art with Jesus on the cross. And when thou hearest severe and improper words, then it is given thee to drink as a medicine of thy soul out of the cup of thy heart.

83. Be still and drink the cup of health to stop revilers and to follow the example of Christ, who was dumb before Pilate, when they testified falsely against Him.

84. Man does not know how good and virtuous he is when he is afflicted with calamity.

85. A true lover fears not to endure pain, scorns not to be of the reviled, if he may only be like Christ in the scandal of the cross. Then to him, to whom Christ is the life, is suffering and death for the sake of Christ great gain.

86. Blessed is the soul that most ardently loves Jesus.

87. A cautious self-examination, is everywhere necessary. Frequent prayer is a sure defence. The silence of the lips is a habitation of peace.

88. Many begin ardently, but constancy gains the crown of bravery.

89. Our sweet Jesus makes all sweet and light.

90. A sensual man seeks ever for ease; a spiritual one always avoids and hates such pleasures.

EJACULATION. It displeases Thee, O my God, when one goes to beg of the frail creature for consolation. Therefore Thou directest me inwardly, and commandest that I wait upon Thee.

91. Just as a proud man enjoys his honor, a rich man enjoys his riches, so a humble man divests himself in his humility, and the spiritually poor in the insignificancy of things.

92. Nothing satisfies the hungry soul, like God Himself who created him, esteem, and all that he thinks, does and says, God records all exactly.

95. A man's greatest triumph is to overcome what diverts him, to tread down what terrifies him, and gently to endure what pains him.

96. To obey quickly, to labor industriously, to shun gadding abroad, to love solitude, makes a devoted and a quiet mind.

97. Wouldst thou be great in heaven, be pure in the world. Justify thyself not before man, his praise is vain.

98. He who is patient, and keeps silence overcomes his calamities, by the service of love.

99. He is mighty in strength, who opposes himself valiantly to vice. He is of a great heart who overcomes his evil desires. He is a brave and well armed soldier, who ventures on with the weapons of moderation. He is held worthy to sit with the angels of heaven, who lives pure on earth.

100. The humble and the pure will overcome the devil.

EJACULATION. Draw me, Lord, then will I begin ardently to run after Thee. I have need of an attraction, even of a great attraction. For when Thou drawest not, no one comes, no one follows, because each is bent down to himself. But draw Thou and see? I come, see! I haste, I run, I burn. Thou hast said, When I am exalted above the earth, I will draw all men after Me. Draw me after Thee, good Jesus, that I may not be alone, but that we may all follow in the savor of Thine anointing. Draw me after Thee leave me not to follow another. We must thereby not become proud, but must together humbly trust, that not in our own strength have we begun and followed on, but by the savor of Thine anointing. When the Father draws, man follows Thee and forsakes himself. Amen.

01. Who is pure from sin; that is a good man; for when the sinner becomes adorned externally, within, he is yet black.

02. Thou art my praise, O God, forever. The sense receiveth not, the understanding reacheth not, how glorious God is in His saints, how wonderful is His majesty.

03. Continue to stand in the truth, So shall the truth make you free from all unrighteousness.

04. When you consider of your own wants, you begin to think a little of different conduct.

05. Shut the door of thy house, so shalt thou have peace.

06. Many, whose affairs do not prosper with them, leave off praying and resisting ; notwithstanding virtue is not attained but by labor and fighting, nor preserved but by circumspection.

07. He is a false and foolish servant who boasts on account of his master's possessions, and despises another's.

108. Everyone is a sufficient burden to himself. What profit is it now to you to mingle in external business and to receive ore than you are able to bear?

109. A man falls away sometimes openly, or he errs or neglects, and thus brings shame on others. So much the more ought be to humble himself. Learn compassion, come to the erring with aid, and by thine own fall, taught wisdom by experience, say to thyself, he is a man and not an angel; as it happened to him, it happened to me, we are brethren.

110. A constant purpose always to do good and always to serve God is an everlasting sacrifice upon the altar of the heart for he who always does good, always prays.

EJACULATION. This is my great blessing that I may honor and serve Thee without reward; fearing no loss, nor bringing any avarice with my love to Thee, for the soul pleases Thee that loves purely. O happy is the one united to Thee alone in life and in death, of God, as to the highest end of happiness, that God may be all in all.

112. He who gladly hears trifles and talks unprofitably, sells his soul for an insignificant price.

113. Fly in all troubles and trials to prayer, as to a

safe haven of the soul, and the sooner the better.

114. God often gives a perception of inward loveliness to the devoutly praying, to those remaining in solitude and in silence, which he refused to the babbling and those roving abroad.

115. He who wishes to hear good new intelligence, hears Christ talk of the kingdom of God.

116. He collects little fruit from many words, who does not examine his heart in prayer, concerning sinful thoughts.

117. A pious soul has he, who examines close every beginning of uncleanliness, leaves nothing to hide in the concealment of the heart which offends the eye of his heavenly Father.

118. O how pleasant and good to him to whom it is given, to adhere to God, and to enjoy Him in secret!

19. The fire of love knows not to be governed by measure, but flies on wings above all the lights of heaven, there he finds his only Beloved, and the Cretor of all things who rules over all, that he in Him may rest most happily, joyful and safe.

20. Let us not be left to trust in ourselves, let us not be highrninded, not seek our own convenience, but

in all submit and subdue ourselves to the human arrangements of God, — with true love for the sake of God. From love, God came into the world and from love, He will draw us again to heaven.

EJACULATION. O infinite intense love of the true Son, through many years and days of poverty, Thou hast supported me freely. Shine often on me, prepare me a dwelling place, till I begin my eternal day. O how sweet and acceptable will Thy presence be, since already, and of such weak, small recollections, such great consolations follow.

121. Love is never idle, she works great and high things, she condescends cheerfully to the lowly and despoiled, she works with diligence what is honorable, and she exercises herself with eagerness, when some trifling thing is commanded her; she has no aversion to touch the infirmity of a wound, to wash feet, to clean clothes, to wipe off dirt.

122. O how blessed is the pure soul, whose all is God, who sees nothing to be desired so precious besides God, but all else appears bitter and burdensome.

123. God seeks after and loves such an one as despises and rejects himself and all things for the sake of his love.

124. A pure soul goes quick and freely to God; and he who on earth desires no ease or honors, flies upwards above all created things of this world.

125. The love of Christ looses all the bands of the world, makes all the burdens light, and the lively spirit comprehends clearly all which is pleasing to God.

126. Be not idle in private, nor babbling in the world; thus shall sin be overcome of silence and flee, for it hates a laboring and silent man, one who prays and reflects on divine things.

27. We who are called of God, are of one mind, redeemed with one price, and watered by the Spirit. He commands us to work with diligence, to love and serve one another, if in truth we wish to serve Christ.

28. . O beloved brother, endure, and thou shalt be sustained against thyself, and thou shalt be exculpated. Have compassion, so shall mercy be bestowed on thee.

29. Often there is a little thing, by which one is exceeding tried in himself, or tormented by another. Such things come to pass by the just permission of God, that so thou mayst discern, that as thou canst not subdue little things thou wouldst not be able to surmount difficult things.

130. Be kind to thy unfortunate brother, and pay for his; afflictions as for thyself; thy good is my good, and thy evil is my evil through compassion.

EJACULATION. I find no heavier burden, than long to wander in the world alienated from Thee, O God! Then I labor in love, and seek no other consolation. I have some distinct perception learnt, that the soul cannot be satisfied with present enjoyments, and that true holiness cannot be retained without communion with Thee.

131. He who reproves another, and prays not for him, or does not pity him, is a merciless enemy — not a kind physician but a troublesome empiric.

132. God who governs and honors all, suffers not his sheep long to go astray defenceless, but drives them back, either striking them with the rod of fear, or brings them to Himself looking upon them with the eyes of love.

133. The fruit of a devout prayer is this, that one unites his heart with God, through the fervent love of the Holy Spirit. He prays most devoutly, who shuts out from himself all vanities.

135. True contrition of heart from the mouth of a humble sinner, is a great cry in the ears of God.

36. He robs himself of eternal happiness and honor, who devotes himself to himself, and not to God as his highest good.

37. He who bears patiently his allotted burden, bears the crucified Jesus upon his shoulders.

38. He who brings an angry man to peace, prepares for Jesus a blooming rest in his soul.

39. He who bears and excuses pious deficiencies of another, will soon obtain mercy from Jesus.

40. He who conceals the shame and offences of another, covers the naked limbs of Jesus with garments.

EJACULATION. Thou judges rightly, O my God, how gladly would I be near Thee, and I cannot sufficiently express how I long for Thee. And I pray this, not only in misfortune, but though I wish it may always be well with me here, I wish rather that I may be with Thee.

41. He who examines his little chamber, and is silent, he lives with Jesus in his bosom.

42. He that prays constantly and ardently in trouble and temptation, will with Jesus fight the good fight of death with Satan.

143. He that entirely gives up all his desires, fulfills with Jesus the will of the Father and bears the cross up the hill Golgatha.

145. He that keeps his heart pure and peaceful, wraps up Jesus in a clean linen cloth, and buries Him in his bosom.

146. A blessed soul, whose life is Christ and that is sure to die with Jesus!

147. He that desires to live to Christ, must crucify himself to Him. He to whom Christ is to be pleasant and sweet, must forsake all things perishable. There is perhaps trouble in the abandonment, and pain in the death, but there follows eternal salvation and life, when one can devise to live holy with Christ.

148. O when shall it be that God shall be all in all to me, that I shall rely entirely on Him, and be united to Him?

149. He that seats a brother by a better table than himself, entertains Jesus with the bread of life and with honeycomb.

150. The royal way to come to Christ is to overcome thine own will, to endure want, not to seek the comfort of the flesh.

Ejaculation. My God, Thou art God above all and I am but a poor insignificant child of man among these lower things. Thou only, art the highest. I am a poor beggar. Heaven is not so far from the earth, as I am separated and removed from Thee. Who will join me to Thee? Thou must do it, for no one else can. When Thou choosest, soon will it come to pass. Thou knowest that of myself I am fit, but to die, to Thee it is given that I stand and go forward. Therefore my soul depends upon the regard of Thy Spirit and the influence of Thy sanctifying grace. When Thou commandest, my soul is raised above the earth. When Thou hidest Thy face, then my soul falls back to itself. Nevertheless on account of Thy love and goodness, Thou wilt accept me and with Thine own right hand draw me to Thee.

51. Let there be no distinction between the great and small, between the rich and poor, the strong and the weak, the wise and the simple, the ruler and the subject, but let us all together praise God who has formed all His creatures with wonderful beauty and diversity for the praise and honor of His name and the honor of mankind.

52. For all the favors God bestows on thee He requires nothing. Yet nothing is so acceptable to Him, as that thou shouldst purely and cordially love and praise Him for His own sake.

153. In all thou dost have God before thy eyes. Be careful that thou do not offend Him.

154. It is a great gain to the soul, when one thinks little of himself, but ascribes all good to God.

155. It is a great act, as well as a great virtue, to be able to distinguish between good and evil. Therefore, O my soul, in thine heart, through all time by day and by night, praise Zion Thy God; so shall thy reward be exceedingly great from God in heaven and upon the earth. All things shall serve thee, both the prosperous and the adverse, the good and the bad, the joyful and the afflicting.

156. A true lover of God, loves God purely, that is, God as God, he loves Him alone, not on account of the advantage which he derives from Him, but entirely for His enduring goodness, and excellent worth.

157. Blessed is he who performs all his actions for the sake of God and His pleasure, from true love with a pure design, and who in all his thoughts directs them to the praise honor and glory of God. Blessed is he who holds himself as nothing, but freely gives up to God, all that he has received.

158. Blessed is he who accepts the rod of affliction, like Job as from the hand of his divine Master, and

offers and gives up himself entirely to the divine will.

59. Blessed is he, who seeks how to please God, who thinks lightly of pleasures, and when he is offended becomes the more joyful, esteeming all temporal injuries for the good of his soul in infirmities that come upon thee for the sake of God. Bear patiently the cross with Jesus, and die daily at the cross for thine eternal salvation. Then, all afflictions of the flesh, if endured with patience, will be a medicine to the soul.

EJACULATION. Let this, O Lord, be my consolation in the place of my pilgrimage, that I am mindful of Thy name and Thy very great love, and that I possess Thee a very present trust. It would become insupportable to live, had I not, Lord, my hope in Thee. Therefore I wish not to enjoy the world, when I should remain without consolation or peace; therefore, I have chosen to rest my joy in Thee.

61. He walks with God in light, who longs to possess nothing of this world, but has fixed his heart on God.

62. He who has whatever he wishes, will be wretched and needy unless he has God for his friend. But he has God who loves him and examines his word.

163. Turn away from things that distract thee, for thou wilt not find, unless thou search thy heart, and seek God above all other good, and love Him sincerely.

164. Why dost thou wish to know what is appointed to another, and forgetting thyself in many things? See! He who knows best to humble himself, and to confide in the will of God, enjoys the most peace; to him all burdens become light for the sake of God, whom he has at heart.

165. Blessed is he, who converses with God in prayer, and passes by in silence, the foreign things that come to pass in the world.

166. Remain in peace and endure a little for the sake of God who will release thee from all burdens and disquiet.

167. The patient and meek, makes always his enemy his friend, and finds always that God is favorable to him.

168. He wanders well and safe who bears Jesus in his heart.

169. Blessed is the pilgrim who seeks no continuing city in this world.

70. O happy men, and wise virgins, who have forsaken all for the sake of Christ, and are constantly proceeding in the only way to your everlasting home.

EJACULATION. Lord, I would serve Thee in all that I do, write, think, say, or learn, and let all my works from the commencement, be furnished in and through Thee. What Thou hast given me, that never take away, — from where the stream cannot run, draw me back again to Thee. Nothing is more acceptable to Thee, or more sweet to me, than when I sincerely ascribe to Thee anything I have done or thought that was right.

71. Tell me, good brother, what leads thee for the sake of holiness to run here and there, to see and hear everything, and not know how to attain to the kingdom of heaven? Blessed is he who guards himself from all wanderings of heart and life, and soon returns to himself with sighs and prayers for grace.

72. He has great peace, who cheerfully remains in his chamber and burns with God in secret, and prays,and reads Christ diligently, and devotes himself to holy contemplations.

73. When it is not salutary and profitable to our souls to endure and be afflicted in the world, God does not permit afflictions to come to pass, for He is

exceeding kind and just in all His ways.

174. Blessed is the servant that employs all his time profitably, and is indifferent to outward objects that do not concern him, and for the sake of God, is become as one deaf and dumb, who goes through the world of tumult peaceful and bears his soul always before him in his hands.

175. To be retired and to be silent is good for peace of heart, and for obtaining a devout prayerfulness. It is a great aid to this to have a secret spot, removed from the tumult where there is no noise.

176 He that speaketh presumptuously is laughed at and despised by many; but he that shall modestly refrain from speaking, meriteth the favor of them that stand by.

177. He must be very strong and well guarded, who walks among men, and is not distracted within by the passing events. Therefore remain in solitude and at home, for the sake of devotion.

178. It must be a very edifying remark that improve on silence. Therefore he has great peace, who guard his lips, remains at home, and prays often.

179. Fly the crowd, live in solitude, follow humility and devoutness, and bear patiently one who is

troublesome, for the sake of Christ who is crucified for you.

180 It is a great humility of heart to think poorly of yourself, and always better of others.

EJACULATION. Lord, when wilt thou take away all hindrances from my heart? Thou true peace, thou highest blessedness, and perfect happiness. O, when without any impediment of opposing forces, can I follow thee safely and freely where thou goest?

181. The pure and discreet guards his heart and his mouth, and all his passions, (which always are inclined to sense) whereby he never sins, or offends God or his friends.

183. Because thou hast not Jesus enwrapped in thine heart, thou seekest often for external consolation. That is weak and useless, and helps little to ease the pain that oppresses thee within.

84. There is great liberty to the confiding soul that has nothing of its own in the world, but for the sake of the kingdom of God, and the of pain for us.

85. Blessed is he who increases his virtues from his necessities and infirmities, and in all that he endures, follows the will of God.

186. Seek for help in God, and God alone, who will always be a joy to thee. All other consolation is nothing. It endures not, it enriches not, however bright it may shine.

187. Choose Jesus Christ the Son of God, for thy particular friend and neighbor, and forsake all for the sake of Christ.

188. That many have many doubts, is not the fault of the Holy Scriptures, but by reason of the blindness of their hearts. Sometimes to the devout man, mysteries are revealed in prayer that to the splendid, and hair splitting speculators, remain concealed.

189. He admonishes well and rationally who applies to himself first, what he observes and condemns in others.

190. There can nowhere be found true rest and safe joy, but in God, in true humility and good patience by which all calamities shall be overcome; therefore, place all thy expectation in God, but not in any creature, be it small or great, for without God all is vanity and with God all is good.

Ejaculation. Sustain me, O dearest God on account of Thy mercy, then soon in Thy strength will all mine enemies come to nought, for with but one word, in an instant are they put to flight by Thee. Ye still for my part must I ever stand in fear, and never rely upon myself, for there shall I be variously distracted and removed from Thee. Upon no feeling, no retirement, no hope can I rely but upon Thy mercy. O sweet compassionate Lord, I am a burden and a hindrance to myself, but with Thee I am strong and free and mighty in myself.

91. He who desires to serve God is gladly alone and prays, but he who wanders out and desires to be talking here and there, it seldom happens that he does not defile himself and comes back to his chamber undevout.

92. The truly humble seeks no praise of his own works, but ascribes all good to God and his sins to himself.

93. A well instructed and intelligent mouth is as vessel of solid gold, filled with ointment scented with balsam and worthy of all honor.

94. It is not a great art or virtue to teach or to punish others, but to govern thyself well and patiently to receive punishment and thereby to improve thyself is great wisdom with God and man.

95. The devout and the humble need few words lest the heart become distracted thereby.

196. It is a great honor when on proves humble in everything and esteems himself small in comparison with others and desires to serve for the sake of Christ, who said, I am under thee as one that serves thee.

197. It is a great art to learn to be silent when you are punished, and great wisdom, to talk understandingly in proper season. It is difficult to men to tarry in every word and work, to observe a limit and to examine themselves. Therefore the loving devout soul wishes to remain in retirement and be still; to flee turmoil and be instant in prayer.

198. Blessed is the soul that often thinks of the last hour, when all things of this life shall come to an end, all joys and sorrows, all honors and shame. Blessed is the soul, though poor, that is become an alien for the sake of God; that despises all the honors of this world, great and magnificent as they may seem to be.

199. Blessed is he who despises the world, and all in the world that can allure to sin, and flies with Elias into the wilderness, because of their great danger.

200. He is much deceived, and is unwise of heart, who desires to live be saluted devoutly, loved deeply, and forever esteemed by all creatures. O inestimable Jesus! How can I show honor to Thee,

or what thanksgiving shall I bring to Thee, who hast shown me infinite mercy? And when I ever find that, would give to Thee, lo, it is already Thine, before give it Thee. How shall I recompense Thee? How shall I render thanks and praise to Thy most holy name? I am now bound to too many things, and unfit for the most trifling service. Yet I will, notwithstanding, my sweetest Jesus, read of Thee, write of Thee, sing of Thee and think of Thee, talk of Thee, labor for Thee and suffer for Thee. I will rejoice in Thee, I will praise Thee, I will magnify Thee, I will glorify Thee, I will worship Thee for Thou art my God, in whom I have trusted, whom I have loved, whom I have sought, whom I have always desired. Give me token that I shall one day see Thy lovely countenance in heaven. Amen.

01. One reads of many fathers who have lived so long. "And he has been, and he has been, and he has been, and so with the rest;" and finally is the conclusion, "and he is dead." For we must all die and become as water spilt upon the ground, from whence we are taken.

02. When you always carry Jesus in your heart, and truly love Him, and daily pray to Him, then will you freely have a living expectation of that kingdom, of which He says, " Father I will, that where I am there shall my servant be."

203. There is no more beautiful employment, or more delightful labor than to love and praise God, thy Creator, and thy Redeemer, with thy whole heart, thy whole soul, thy whole mind, and with all thy strength.

204. Cleave to God according to the best of thy ability and knowledge, always readily and purely, that God may be all in all, be loved and praised, before all, and above all by thee, and thou be exalted and made happy with him through all eternity.

205. Cease not to pray and to praise God. If thou often neglect, thou sinnest and offendest Him; despair not, however, but be so much the more devout, and beg for love for thus wilt thou be beloved; then love repairs all past evil.

206. Give thyself up to God, and all that thou hast; give Him all that thou dost know, and art able to do, thus mayst thou become as rich and beloved of God as thou hast been.

207. He has given me such grace that I must do all to the praise and honor of the Lord my God, and do all things as just as I possibly can. Nothing, be it small or great, must draw, bend, trouble, or at all hinder me from serving God. But perhaps it is not possible that at present I can attain thereto, yet all things are possible with God, who in love can unite

the devout soul with him through grace.

208. He who loves Christ has peace and tranquillity, and desires nothing else besides Him; the peace of the trusting soul is in this love, to bear adversity for the sake of the love of God, and the name of Christ. He that proposes and designs otherwise, is deceived and in error.

209. The peace that Christ teaches and promises, consists in deep humility, in loathing of one's own will, in the destruction of all sinful inclinations, and the shunning of all worldly praise and external trust in temporary things.

210. Examine thy heart within, and thy wishes without, lest thou shouldst be captivated by any amusement to the injury of thy soul.

EJACULATION. Stand by me, most gracious God, keep me near Thee, lest I begin to winder from Thee, and become removed from the highest good, which Thou, O Lord, art; for in Thee alone is my good. Give me Thyself, then hath my soul enough, Lord God my salvation. Amen.

211. They are foolish and thoughtless, who seek things temporal, and hold for great that which cannot satisfy the soul, nor grant tranquillity.

212. Everything of this world is deficient and inconstant. Nothing is perfect out of God, nor to be esteemed our highest enjoyment, or best good.

213. Direct not thy thoughts or thy longing, on any living creature or beautiful idol, or high station, if thou wouldst not be deceived, disquieted, distracted; for all is vain, slippery, and injurious, when thou dost not direct all to God, from whom is all good, and in whom all things are and exist.

214. In all thy thoughts, conversations and actions, have always a clear view of the presence of God. See Him in the beginning and end of all thy doings, lest thou lose the fruit of thy labor.

215. What shouldst thou know, and wherein shoulds thou trust and hope? Not in thyself, nor in man, nor in anything of the world, nor in the stars of heaven, but alone in God, thy Creator, who made thee, and holds thee and all creatures alike in his hand and power, without complaint or helper.

216. Pray for all and commend all to God. Be little in thine own eyes, that thou mayst be great in the eyes of God.

217. He is not without praise and honor, who despises all praise and honor for the sake of God. He is not without holy consolation, who regards all the joy

of this world as nothing and for the sake of Christ
endures all adversity.

218. Blessed is he who follows Jesus in his life, in
patience and the cross; for in the end, it shall be well
to him with Jesus, and he will not presume to fear,
that He will not hear him in the day of trouble.

219. That soul is unwise, and will always be poor
and miserable, that seeks and loves anything besides
God, and that separates its heart from the honor and
love of God.

220. Love Me, says the Lord, then shall you not be
cast down. All the trouble of temporal poverty become light in the fire of love. To the loving soul it
is sweet, to become poor with the Son of God, all
burden is light, that love commands us to bear, and
no labor is painful strengthened by the bread of love.

EJACULATION. O Lord, esteem me worthy to
be with Thee, for I would gladly go, Lord, for Thy
sake I have begun, for Thy sake I have given up the
world, for Thy sake I endure temptation, for Thy
sake have I taken this labor upon me, and for Thy
sake I die daily, and for Thy sake I am counted a
fool, and useless man. Lord! Accept Thy servant
through grace, then shall I not fear, what flesh or
man can do.

221. From this time will I consider for my riches, poverty; for mine honor, humility; for my peace, patience. For these things will I care and those things only shall delight me that the spirit seeks and that do not profit the flesh. In these things will I find joy equally as in other riches. I will rejoice in the Lord, cheerfully cast myself on God, my Jesus, who has become a pattern of humility, poverty and patience.

222. When a humble man is reproved or accused, he seeks for no apology, or rejoinder, but receives all with submission, confesses his guilt, and promises better; and why this? Because he seeks not to please men, but to please God.

223. They wish much to be devout but do not wish to suffer insults; they desire humility, but with the humble, wish not to be despised of men. They wish to love the virtuous, without hating the vicious.

224. Jesus says: Mortify, my children, mortify your own wills, your own sight, your own designs and judgments, and all sins of the flesh. Mortify these enemies or you become as dead. Mortify your own heart, return to God. Hope in Him alone.

225. One says, I hast a little peace; but I say thou hast not peace, because thou art so full of selfishness, because thou art so fleshly, because thou walkest in worldly wisdom.

226. He does unwisely, who acts against his conscience, and offends God for the sake of the devil.

228. Who has vexation in praying, or desire to trifle, who is full of ardor? Surely none; for when within one becomes fervent, he would avoid all vain talking.

229. Return to thine own heart, return to God, who created thee. Hope in him and he will sustain thee. If thou canst not serve him with a sound mind, serve him with a weak mind, then shall he crown thee with roses and lilies, with the sainted martyrs in heaven.

30. One should at all times watch, and in all places be very cautious, that the devil does not deceive him, and find him unarmed.

EJACULATION. Lord Jesus, be Thou my refuge, and my only consolation. Be Thou my only friend, for all my friends have forsaken me. Be Thou my hope, for the hope of man is vain. Be Thou the joy of my heart, for the joy of this world is entirely vanity. Be Thou my teacher, friend and companion, in this road on which I travel.

31. Observe circumspectly, what images are suggested to thee, whether of the world or of the flesh, and shut the door of thy heart, that Satan may not enter. O thou most blessed friend of God, observe

warily, the artful and fatal suggestions of the devil, that he may not draw thee away to himself, but as soon as thou feel the prohibited movements, avert your mind, call upon the name of the Lord, and weep on account of the evil suggestions.

232. Fear therefore, O thou proud man, the judgmen of God in all thy actions; and take care not to boast for any vain reputation thou mayst assume to thyself. When thou shalt have done all that thou canst, and art obliged to, yet dost thou still fail in many things, and art hardly able to give account for one of a thousand. Fear then the rod of God, fear His staff, fear the judgment to come.

233. Stand in the fear of God, and watch always for the beginning of temptation, and pray with sighing of heart, in the spirit of humility, of good thou dost, or learnest, ascribe not to thine own industry or labor, but entirely to His holy grace and mercy.

234. No one fears and flies the devil so much, as one who is humble and despises himself. And upon no one has he so much influence as the highminded, and upon him who much esteems himself.

235. As long as thou livest, thou must strive against the wiles of the devil, and thine own passions. Now and then he leaves thee a little time, in the

exercise of his cunning, that when thou art free and unarmed, he may fall upon thee suddenly whilst thou art unmindful.

236. We who are named of Christ should dissuade our minds from all fascinating visible things, and raise ourselves to the contemplation of the invisible objects of our Creator.

237. A true servant of God guards diligently his ways, and checks the extravagances as well of nature as of love, that he may not forsake the highest good, which he cannot retain together with temporal things. But as soon as he feels distracted and hindered, he should go again by prayer to God.

238. He is truly watchful, and holds not the name of Christ in vain, who is dead to the world, and lets it be his delight to live to Christ; who aims all his thoughts and works to God as the end; who desires to possess no self-love nor self-indulgence, but sacrifices himself, with all of good he looks for in heaven or on earth and comes to God the highest good with continual contemplation, from whom comes and flows out all created good.

239. It belongs to one under good subjection to improve the commands with joy, and to do nothing of his own will, but after the example of Christ, to give himself willingly into the hands of God, for this is

the most acceptable gift, one can offer God, and O how precious is the perfection of Christ's love that some can stand secure before God in spite of the upbraidings of former transgressions. He that chooses possessions and retains this, he goes the short way to the heavenly home that Adam and Eve lost by disobedience, but that Christ has through his obedience again obtained for us.

240. Hold this for an important truth, when you have nothing of your own wisdom, that he who prefers simple obedience to syllogisms and his own notions, he who does this, pleases God.

EJACULATION. Write, O Jesus, Thy words on my heart, and grant that I with desire may be patient of insult and wrong, that it may be done to me as Thou wilt that in life or in death I may be fashioned like Thee. Be Thou my life, then shall death be to me great gain.

241. He that desires to obtain the greatest growth, acts up to a diligent obedience in all things. A delighting and pure obedience, that waits not for long arguments, but fulfills commands without complaint is a great and excellent virtue.

242. The strongest art of overcoming, is to overcom thyself perfectly, and to despise thyself on account of thy obedience.

243. Stand always upon the watch of thy heart, and return soon within. For where thou hast not peace within, it shall not be well with thee, thou mayest externally and earthly conceal what thou wilt.

244. It causes much peace, and examination of heart when thou conductest worldly affairs with regularty, for thus everything is done in its time and with deliberation.

245. These things must one bear patiently, viz. poverty of this world's goods, the insults of enemies, the distresses of life, the customs of the unpolished, hard words, the withdrawal of consolation, by which man is proved as if purified in the fire. And when this ffliction is rightly used, it shall prove to him, great growth in holiness.

46. Many know what to do and what to avoid, but the flesh will not turn to the examination of the heart and mouth, whereby through some trifling circumstance, they are drawn to their accustomed vices.

47. There is perpetual peace to the humble: but the proud and the temptation, one must daily fight, holding an unmoved mind, and standing in godly graces all the stage of this slippery life, and inward conflict is ended.

49. Thou shouldst watch and consider much about

thine heart, what thoughts and inclinations thou feelest, that thou mayest drive away evil and receive the good, as David says, — I bear my soul always in mine hands, I never forget thy law.

250. To increase purity of heart, solitude and tranquillity much contribute, and also to read, and pray, and to wish to know nothing of the condition of the world.

EJACULATION. My soul depends upon Thee and loves Thee above all gifts, fair and sweet as they may be, that Thou out of Thy love preparest for me. Thou alone art the bridegroom; other things are bridal presents and love tokens. I will not love nor trust in the same instead of Thee, so as to let them satisfy me without Thee, lest I lose both them and Thee. Thou lettest us use many things on thy account, but Thou wouldst have us choose nothing instead of Thee. Therefore have I chosen Thee, my beloved bridegroom Jesus Christ, before all other things, and I would seek to love Thee above all other things. So, grant then, that I may enjoy happiness with Thee, and in future union with Thee, partake of eternal bliss. Amen.

251. Guard well thy mouth, for thou must give an account of every unprofitable word. He who guards not his tongue, his religion is vain, for if he guards it not, it originates much sin, of which a still

man is free. Therefore, be silent, refraining from useless conversation, for a babbler loses his devoutness, begets disorder, misspends time, forgets conscience, and offends others.

252. When thou wouldst have tranquillity, avoid public places, and withdraw to retirement that thou mayest pray.

253. Many, because they have not examined their little chamber are thrown by various circumstances into the world and unfortunately perish. Ah, shame that we are not able to hold out long enough till we have produced ripe fruit from ourselves.

254. Every man should behave himself as if he should daily die.

255. Think, that God and thou art alone in the world, so shalt thou have great peace of mind.

256. He that "desires to know" heavenly mysteries, must guard himself from society. Thus Moses, when about to receive the law, withdrew himself from the tumult of the world to remain with the Lord on the mountain.

257. When thou art able to overcome indolence, and restrainest thy heart from wandering, thou treadest the way of piety, and soon shall enjoy holiness for-

ever.

258. A devout singer and prayer regards and attends but to God and himself.

259. After prayer and singing, engage not immediately in temporal affairs, lest thou lose the grace that thou hast obtained through prayer. Much rather shouldest thou gather the fruits of prayer and praise and remain in quiet. For that devotion soon disappears that the discipline of tranquillity has not proved.

260. All things are to be borne patiently, as the loss of property, vexations of enemies, sickness, incivilities, severity of speech, want of consolation, the affection of friends; by the sea man is proved and is as if purged in the fire. Come to me, all ye who labor.

EJACULATION. O Lord, to Thee I flee, teach me Thy will, and learn me to give up my own. Therein consists everything that I should learn to say, — O Father, Thy will he done. Nothing is better or more salutary for my soul. Thou Lord, art all my good, Thou art my teacher, Thou art my book, for without Thee I should be unlearned and unprofitable for all things.

261. It is no trifling sin in the presence of God and the holy angels, to stand with a doubting heart.

262. In all undertakings, to a trusting soul, there is no such useful labor, or so acceptable service to God, as devoutly to pray, and to praise God with a whole heart offering.

263. God asks not for the destruction of love, but the overcoming of vice.

264. He that wishes to run today, and tomorrow to bear a burden, goes not forward in God's way. To-day, we wish for nothing and tomorrow we wish to take more than enough. This is not, to love to poverty, but to strengthen covetousness.

265. Wouldst thou seek God with singular grace, then consider, that thou art a man and not an angel, that the grace is given to thee, and not innate.

266. When in temporal things thou perform thy duties, lay not open thyself entirely to visible objects, but often devote thyself in prayer to God. What is outwardly seen should sustain us to serve God, but not hinder us.

267. God is the blessedness of the soul. By no innate goodness is the soul that comprehends it, heavenly, and a stranger to this world. Love hates vice, condemns sensuality, persecutes sin, restrains the force of nature, and would overcome what is contrary to God and virtue.

269. Dost thou wish to have love of God, and peace with the brethren? Break thine own will, do not appear with exaltation, but humble thyself in every part of thy conduct.

270. The more one overcomes himself and improves his deficiencies, the better will the love of God grow in him, and the reign of the flesh be weakened.

EJACULATION. Lord, Thou knowest all my weaknesses, and my great ignorance, and the daily unsteadiness of my affections to Thee, that so quickly I fly here and there, and often wander far away. Lord, be gracious to me, according to the abundance of Thy mercy, and draw me again to Thee. Hold my heart to Thee, in devout prayer and holy contemplation, day and night, as much as is possible in this infirm love.

271. The deficiency of things should teach us to prize poverty. Moderation in the midst of pleasure is a rare virtue.

272. A pious soul should guard itself from the bonds of the body, for flesh draws flesh; to love the beautiful and to desire the effeminate, belongs not to the virtue of chastity. The more the flesh is oppressed, the higher will the spirit rise.

273. He that considers his body as the prison of his

soul, will not care to ornament it, and therefore, to be attracting notice, for soon it will return to dust and corruption.

274. He is not worthy to be trusted of God, who lusts for transitory things, and groans about his wants.

275. Chastity has many adversaries, but to be truly humble and to seek God diligently for help, to watch carefully the passions, will obtain the victory, under the teaching of Jesus Christ.

276. The surest way of perfection, of illumination of the mind, and of introduction to eternal life, is to become conformed to the virtues and example of Christ.

277. Learn to direct and ordain all your exercises to the love and honor of Christ, and see Jesus present in all places and at all times.

278. This is to have Christ dwell in thy heart with confidence and love, never to turn thy eyes from contemplation of Him, to aim at his pleasure always, and to prefer nothing to His love.

279. Become like the all holy Jesus, imitate His poverty, humility, patience, and contempt of this world,

280. He lives rightly and lives holy, to whom Christ is all in all, and loved more than all, who dwells more in Christ than in himself, who thinks nothing of himself, but sweetly and joyously reposes his hope in Christ.

EJACULATION. Lord Jesus, come and cleanse me, wash me and wipe me, that I may be accepted of Thee, with a pure heart and chaste life, for nothing is good without thee.

281. They will be found to have lost little who fix their desires on eternity, and desire nothing of earthly honors or gratifications.

282. He that burns with the love of Christ, enjoys poverty and contempt, and bends low in humility. He who moderately supplies his discreet wants, and chooses the little, rather than the more, who is a true contemner of the world, and a friend of God, is travelling home.

283. No one will more surely be exculpated than he that knows his own guilt, and humbles himself therefore. If another apologizes for thee, ascribe such excuses to his friendship, rather than to thine own innocence. So long as thou hast not bread, shouldst thou partake with Christ. All kindness shall be recompensed to thee here and hereafter.

285. The avaricious is always poor. He who trusts in God, receives enjoyment from the whole world. Consider that temporal want incurs no spiritual shame, but when earthly bounties fail thee, lose not thereby thy spiritual consolation. Confide deeply in the providence of God. He that has promised things heavenly and eternal, will not deprive of temporal happiness. Lord, Thou art ever with me, and all that have is Thine.

286. Thou wilt be most rational, when thou art most intimate with thine own heart.

287. This is the way of wisdom: that one perform outward things, but forget not the internal—that one have his time of business, (for the things of himself) but remain a stranger to the fascinations of things.

288. Restrain thy external labor and business, that thou mayst apply a part of the day to prayer, and to the reading and contemplation of the Scriptures. When thou canst, allot a period for this purpose, at evening morning and noon.

289. Thou wilt have time enough for holy quiet, when thou usest no time idly, and not only have no idle actions, but no idle thoughts or words.

290. Take diligently the words of thy mouth under thy observation, lest thou say anything thou wouldst

afterwards repent.

EJACULATION. Lovely Jesus, make it as Thou shalt best choose to have it appear to Thee, when I know not myself to be well grounded. To Thee everything is known which is profitable for me. I give up, therefore, myself to Thee—create me according to Thy all lovely will.

291. We often fail in that we justify our deficiences by the examples or conversation of others, even as one is praised, because another did the same.

292. Because thou often hearest various and novel things said sometimes, trust in them not too easily, nor repeat them afterwards to others, for it is better to be silent. What does it profit thee? Follow Christ, and let the dead bury their dead.

293. It is useful for young men and serviceable to young plants, to choose the lowest and meanest places and service, and enjoy themselves in their despising the customs of the world, and become unknown and disesteemed in the eyes of men.

294. He is truly an unhappy man, who makes himself a man of the world, and counts its praise as blame. What has a poor and needy man to fear more than to become esteemed and praised of his fellow men?

295. He that engages in many cares, forgets himself. But he that seeks only the one, that is all in all, will have much peace of conscience.

296. To desire to have all things according to thy own notions, is wrong and impossible. Wouldst thou be a perfect servant of God, obey in all things, not thine own, but the will of God.

297. Do not desire in this or that, that thy will or choice be fulfilled, which is often selfish and wrong; say also, "as the Lord will, so let it be," and then all will be for the best.

298. By this is one known to be a servant of God, who accepts all for good, knowing that the highest perfection consists in cutting off one's will.

299. When one comes to such a depth of self-loathing, that neither in great or small things, neither in prosperity or in adversity does he seek his own will, he can with justice say, "It is finished."

300. Then wilt thou ask much, when with inextinguishable longing of praise thee with as exalted a voice and devout affections, as thou art praised by any creature in heaven or upon earth. I desire to honor Thee with greater and more estimable honor, than Thou art honored by any saint in Thy heavenly kingdom. I would reverence and love Thee,

with such ardent inclinations and loving heart, as the most devout and perfect heart may or can love Thee. The holy and pure passion of Thy love must always burn in me. It must inflame my loins and my heart, as a renewing fire from heaven, and purify and renew me within, that no sin may remain that shall displease the purity of Thy eyes. O, my God, Thou true searcher of my heart, all my desires are to Thee. Amen.

301. This is thy duty, to walk worthy of God, and in temporal business not to divert the mind from those things that are above, but always keep thy mind fixed on heaven and the joys that are to come. How canst thou be so happy as promptly and willingly to meet the inward call of God?

302. To aid one to hold constant friendship with God, it greatly assists that he hold familiar intercourse of heart with Him. But he who desires such privilege should be given him, must avoid unprofitable conversation and business; for the love of Christ cannot be united with an unteachable, dissipated heart.

303. Think well of thy friend, but best of God.

304. One said in his sermon to the multitude: "Our Lord, the Count, is dead. He lived here a little and brief time. He had a yearly rent and income, he has

now lost, and cannot carry it away with him. May he possess that sole remaining inheritance that is to come, that will suit so well to his case." Therefore is he happy, who, poor in possessions and rich in virtue, can say at the end of life, with the confidence of David, "the Lord is my Shepherd, I shall not want."

305. Let the words of Jesus be imprinted on thy heart. Let Jesus be thy guard through all the way. Draw towards him as thy defence and armor, and hold him in thy hand as thy sword and staff.

306. Let all thy hope and joy be in God, and prepare with thy good will to endure all for the sake of God. All the joy of the world passes quickly away, and all its praise is full of bitterness and deceit.

307. He is an unhappy and pitiful man who serves not God. He that loves not God, has forsaken all that he possesses. Ha is vain and ignorant—he fixes his hope upon the creature.

308. He that in things equal or less, has subdued himself, overcomes the devil.

309. He has always joy and peace, who subdues, loathes, exposes, and despises himself; and who, that he may be obedient for the sake of God, freely, of his whole heart, gives up himself to God and mankind through all time.

310. Never have great thoughts of thyself, and despise not the weak, for no one knows how it will turn out with himself, unless he shall remain faithful.

EJACULATION. Ah, dear Lord, make me partaker of Thy grace — forsake me not in my trouble, because I am not more subject to Thee. I have not yet quitted the ground, I am not yet entirely dead to myself, nor am I entirely delivered and freed from inclinations for temporal gratification. Make me whole, dearest Lord, for Thy mercy's sake. Preserve me from my grovelling propensities, and raise me from earth to heaven. Come, Lord Jesus, quickly.

311. Even as thou behavest towards thy brother and neighbor, even so, with just judgment, shalt thou find it afterwards that another condemns thee. The good that thou doest to a weak, trusting, wounded brother, thou doest to Christ.

312. When temptation approaches, thou shouldest immediately pray. Despair not, give not up duty: be firm, and commend thyself to God.

313. How prudent and rational is he, who forsakes the things of the earth, and avoids all occasions to sin, and contemplates on Him, in retirement from worldly tumult.

314. O, how useful and fruitful are his studies, who

exercises himself daily in the life and sufferings of Christ and forsakes those high and vainly curious things that distract from Christ and God.

15. A man of good and perfect will, has always God before his eyes, and always seeks to please God in all his works and thoughts. He loves to see another's progress in holiness of heart and tongue, and esteems him as his own.

16. O! Thou poor, weak, and despised brother, be not weary of affliction. Endure yet a little longer willingly; for he who cannot endure much with joy, how can he pretend to much holiness? Be patient at least under light words, although thou canst not yet endure a hard stroke.

17. Rest not thy hope and peace on man, or on any creature of earth or heaven, if thou wouldst not wander, be deceived, or confounded. Thy safety is alone in living to the highest and truest good, viz: God.

18. Let Jesus be in thine heart, in all places, at all times, in leisure and occupation. Walk, also, without deceit or vexation, as becomes an humble servant of God, who is prepared for all good.

19. Wherever thou art, let devout prayer be to thee thy companion and consolation.

320. Everything here below is frail—everything in the world is vanity, excellent as it may seem to be. In God alone are all good things, perfect and without end. Follow Jesus, despise all things here that thou mayst enjoy all things in Him.

EJACULATION. O, Jesus, Thou true life, Thou undying life, grant that I may be crushed through love, that I may be wounded through love, even that I may die through love. Then shall not the flesh rule it over me.

321. Turn thy heart to the lowly and gracious Jesus; then shall thy soul find consolation, all earthly thing become good, and be transformed to the image of eternal joy.

322. With great earnestness press forward to that which is before; forget what is behind and what appertains to this world, and think not of trouble and infirmity. He who desires to advance must begin anew every day, shun no labor, and let no time pass by unemployed.

323. Many wish to serve God, yet not to endure any hardship, but to live here in all health. They who thus seek, are living with earthly feelings, and do not yet comprehend the spiritual combat of men.

324. Observe for thy caution, what I now say. When

thou dost not wish to be seduced from the way of the Lord — when thou wishest to watch and to remain in the society of the good, avoid the society of worldly thinking men— avoid the situations of temptation, lest thou see and hear the vain things of the world, so that also thou mayst not, when thou engagest in the things of this life with them, be associated with them in feeling.

325. Try to be silent, be tranquil—hide and retire: be glad when thou canst be unknown.

326. He will seldom remain long dutiful, who mingles much with worldly minded people.

327. A light that is shut up in a lanthorn preserves its brightness and fire, but one which is exposed is put out and eclipsed by a slight breeze.

28. He must be very strong and well grounded in virtue, and walk circumspectly in business and conversation, who produces fruit among the multitude, and can live without peril of conscience in the world.

29. The unarmed and weak must seek safe places, for it is very difficult to engage in the bustle of the world and prove free from sin.

30. Flee with the holy Elias from the sight of the

angry woman Jezebel, and go into the wilderness of retirement, and resolve upon a purpose of everlasting forbearance, till apart the tumult of the world, you shall have passed the fiery temptation towards heaven.

Ejaculation. My beloved comes into my heart in order that I may eat of the fruit of his vine. He inclines himself to me—he shows himself to me, and I give up myself to him, for he is my possession and my joy.

331. The heart that is not kept in devout and inward exercise, must necessarily become dissipated.

332. There is no certain way to attain a knowledge of all good, but by the inward working of the Holy Spirit, and the meek and humble person becomes most easily worthy of his anointing.

333. Perhaps this is the last day, perhaps the last hour, perhaps thou wilt not see tomorrow: exercise thy power, neglect not time, the past hour comes not again.

334. Deplore the direct loss of all time not combining the service of God.

335. Exercise thyself continually in prayer, for it is an invincible defence against inimical assaults.

336. O, that thou, not only for one day, but for whole years, mayst be bowed down to God. Ah, thou art too inconstant and distracted or thou wouldst be more devout.

337. Whether thou art at home or abroad, let thy soul be always in thy hands.

338. Examine diligently thy little chamber, then shall it prove thee. A servant of God has no safe place in this world, so that he must hide himself in secret. There he prays to his Father with a free mind, when he has shut the door of this chamber.

339. He that can restrain himself, let him restrain, a real solitary enjoys the kingdom of God in his solitude.

340. The aim of the faithful, is to despise all things earthly, to serve God in purity of heart and government of lips.

EJACULATION. O, eternal, exalted, everlasting God. I am Thy creature—I am made to love Thee—I will love Thee even now; but I cannot love Thee as much as I would, because I am not yet bound up in Thy pure love. O, that Thou mayst soon become sweet and pleasant to me, that I may soon flee to Thee and forget all others.

341. He is brave who despises the world, but he is more brave who overcomes himself, despises all his own doings, and willingly becomes poor for the sake of Christ.

342 Wouldst thou not be distracted, then entangle thyself not with foreign things which are not commanded thee; therefore let also thy mouth be shut.

343. Guard against much gadding, and where thou hast no business, there thou must not go. When obedience demands or usefulness calls, go with proper discipline and return soon again to thy retirement.

344. Let Jesus be always with thee. On the way, in the midst of thy labors, be thou always thinking of thy beloved Jesus, who always sees thee and searches into all hearts.

345. Wouldst thou not be entangled, then look not much round about thee. The eyes, like a director of the senses, fasten soon thy volatile heart. It is difficult to see beautiful things, and in thy seeing not to be distracted. Therewith thou loosest thyself from open or secret restraints. Be rather within than without.

346. Return always to thyself, or become alike polluted and distracted. Seek renewedly to gain in solitude what thou hast lost in public. Ah, one

seldom goes without hazard and seldom does one go home again without self-accusation. Think on God alone.

47. Dust thou art and to dust thou shalt return, and soon be trodden under foot of man. Think of thy last end. See, they all pass away as a shadow, and each goeth to his destruction.

48. In all affairs, inward or outward, that thou art called to undertake, inquire after the pleasure of God, and prefer his honor to thine own profit.

49. When there happens to thee aught adverse or unfortunate, be not terrified with sudden fear, but fly humbly to the Lord who forsakes not those that trust in him.

50. When thou errest within, let not thy soul be faint-hearted nor despairing; when thou, through an injurious libel or sudden passion art overcome, endeavor to apprehend thy fault, know thy mistake, determine to do better, and as for the rest, conduct thyself as thou shouldst.

EJACULATION. O, Jesus, what a sweet thing is thy love; how well it sounds; how lovely it enters; how sure it holds and binds. Ah, that Thou wouldst bind me to Thy everlasting service; make me entirely captive, and may I be Thine alone. Then am I truly free, when a prisoner to Thy love, and am free from all selfishness. Lord, I am Thy servant; Thine I am for Thou hast pursued after me. I am freely Thine, and I am not ashamed that I am thine alone. I wish not to be myself; help Thou that I may be loosed from all selfishness. Blow kindly; wake up a little spark; so shall my heart inflame, and even become purer, clearer, lovelier. Then Thy love shall chase away all vice, and consume all sin. Hold me with the hands of love, then shall my poor services stand firm. Amen.

351. He who desires not honor, seeks nothing useful he goes everywhere forth joyfully, but he who seeks things earthly shall endure grief.

352. So long shall strife be among men as they persevere in their own will. He shall soon be in peace who subjects and subdues himself.

353. None lives so tranquil or dies so safely, as one who is truly obedient and subjected to God and mankind in all things.

354. He who strongly exerts himself for the sake of God, to him shall God give the greater grace, and be shall soon become a perfect man.

355. He is not idle who prays devoutly; it is indeed the greatest labor to be given up to prayer, when one

has no desire for it.

356. Let this be our principal work, always to praise God and to do all our outward and inward duties, small and great, with a pure and upright heart for His honor.

357. Study more to perform the will of another than thine own.

358. Converse little and converse devoutly; it is better to be silent, than to talk without caution. Continue cheerfully in thy little chamber; if thou canst not, then guard thy lips.

359. As often as thou goest out and when thou returnest to thy room, make a short prayer. Employ not thy heart in outward things, but learn to labor with thy hands and to pray with thy heart both at the same time.

360. No one is immediately perfect and true virtue and practice is not acquired in a day; but it is only by daily exercise and industrious intention, that a man becomes ardent and devout.

EJACULATION. May I remember, O Lord, all Thy mercies and all Thy benefits which have been of old, until at last, by the assistance of Thy grace, I merit to arrive safe to Thee. Deliver me from all those evils which rush in suddenly upon me and by which my heart is frequently drawn from the meditation of celestial goods. Be Thou precious with me, O gracious God, and place me near to Thee, lest I begin to wander forth and go away too far from the chief good, salvation. Amen.

361. Now, Lord, I would immediately leave everything for Thy sake; that I may soon find Thee; that Thou may be in me and I in Thee, through love; that Thou mayst inflame me. I pray Thee, Lord, remain free and unhindered with me, lest I forsake Thee, becoming as one banished in prison, and as a pilgrim sinking down by the way.

362. All exercises should so work in us as that the passions and affections may be overcome; that our will may become dead, the world contemned, and God loved.

363. Be not satisfied with only exercising thyself in prayer a little, then shall thou find great tranquillity.

364. The time of our pilgrimage here is short, but there follows a joy which knows no end. Many endure more for the world than we for God.

365. When anything happens adverse or troublesome, external or internal, then especially must we recur to the sufferings of Christ and consider

how much the Lord suffered for us, unworthy as we are, and then shall we be consoled that He has but given us to drink out of His cup.

366. Cast away thy servile fear, and imbibe the spirit of strength and love. Be strong and valiant for they are more that are for us, than they that are against us. Christ, says the Lord, will go before thee, and fight for thee, and be with thee wherever thou goest.

67. Let thy chamber be thy paradise; let tranquility be thy friend; labor thy companion; prayer thy helper.

68. In labor or common society, converse seldom or little. Go seldom out and when thou art called out, soon return again.

69. Be not zealous, but in whatever thou doest, act calmly.

70. By patience and humility, thou canst overcome all adversity.

jaculation. O, thou fountain of friendship and of endless mercy, thou never ceasest to rain from above, but always continuest wide open to those that approach thee. Oh, that all might draw nigh to thee and might enjoy of the pleasures of thy table, for they are greatly to be desired; in them is no death—no bitterness.

371. Blessed is he who has no hope on the earth. Blessed is he who despises all temporal consolation for the sake of Christ. Blessed is he who can endure when forsaken of God and men. Blessed is he who waits the ordinance of God, and accepts all at His hands.

372. Learn to live without human consolation, even when there is abundance of consolation; for thou art not long to be here and man will not continue long with thee. All will soon be forgotten for all worldly things should be nothing and vanity in thine heart.

373. He hears the voice of Jesus, he despises the world, who restrains the flesh, resists the devil, overcomes his propensities and he loves Jesus with his whole heart who imitates him according to his ability.

374. O, man, thou hast no reason to complain or be displeased with anyone so much as with thyself who art disobedient unto God.

375. In all thy actions, prove thy heart and lips, because thou art inclined to evil. For this it best aids, to remain in solitude, to pray, to write, to labor.

376. Be not in labor disquieted for vexation, for

God is the cause of all good works who will give to each his reward in heaven, according to His own good pleasure.

77. Rise up, thou sleeping brother, then shall Christ illuminate thee. Rise up, indolence, Christ calls thee. Rise up quick, there is danger in to overcome and enjoy himself.

78. Ceasest thou to pray and to watch, then begins the enemy to overcome and enjoy himself.

79. A devout brother is a lover of poverty; he seeks solitude, avoids tumult, loves tranquillity, refrains from long conversation, desires to serve God alone, despises all earthly things, longs to be all the time with Christ.

80. He that wishes to overcome sin must often inflict violence upon natural disposition, implore the grace of Christ humbly, and await all patiently.

EJACULATION. O tenderest and best beloved, incline me to Thee as often as Thou seest me, that my inclinations may be drawn from the burden of anything criminal, or held by vain occupations, lest I deviate far from Thee and begin to pursue a host of sinful thoughts and suddenly be deprived of Thy grace and without which I cannot continue in Thine excellent friendship. Thou art my Lord and my God;

Thou healest and sanctifiest with Thy word.

381. Jesus says, Love Me and forsake thyself, then shall thou find Me at all times and all places. I am the highest good that thy soul should most earnestly desire.

382. Jesus says, See, I stand before the door of thy heart and knock. Open and I will enter in, for I am thy salvation and thy life.

383. Jesus says, I am entirely thine, here and everywhere present. But the blind see me not, and the dea hear me not, and the foolish understand me not.

384. Jesus says, Be thou entirely Mine. Seek thyself in nothing and thy God shall taste most dear to thee of all things.

385. Woe, woe, woe, (says the Angel in the Revelation) to those that dwell upon the earth. Woe to fleshly minds which yet live with lust for the world.

386. O dirt! Dirt, how long wilt thou adhere to me? O darkness and drowsiness, how long shall I be entangled with you?

387. Daily experience teaches us, that earthly expectations are deceitful, and will bring bitterness to us all, who live away from God in the days of our

pilgrimage.

388. All my joints say, seek nothing for thyself, for here thou shalt be satisfied with earthly things, thou shalt be consumed.

389. 1 wish not to go abroad, but to die in my bed, and to be buried in my grave. 1 rejoice much that I have found a tomb wherein 1 can sleep, and not see the iniquity upon the earth.

390. In all temporal changes we must regard providence from above, and in contemplation of the providence, throw ourselves down humbly before God, and pray that he would give us what is most serviceable for our God. As the clay in the hands of the potter, so must we be in Thy hands.

EJACULATION. Lord, to serve Thee out of love is most dear, and a consolation in all labor. Love seeks for no profit or ease, fears no discomfort, but seeks Thee with all delight.

91. Observe the grace that is given thee from above and study to live according to the same, for all have not the same conveniences of situation to be alone with Christ, as to thee more than to many others is given convenient and sufficient time. Let only the spirit of Christ be in thee, that teaches and enlightens every man that comes into the world. Then when

this spirit is in thee, thou needest not to seek any man for the sake of consolation.

392. He enjoys himself, who has arrived so far that it is sweet to him to live without any human consolation, for he seeks the external less, the more abundantly he is consoled within by the spirit.

393. Despise not another, who needs yet more of external consolation; perhaps it is good to him that thou createst a little breeze. But thou ascendest a little higher, and be surely so far compassionate towards another, that thou imitate not his weakness.

394. It is truly a laudable way of perfection to external life, not only in peace, but in adversity and temptation, to praise and love God.

395. Without permission of the Creator, dare one begin to love the creature? But after the will of the flesh is therein diverted, from such the influence of the spirit is withdrawn.

396. See the beautiful form of the bridegroom, and contemplate the worthiness of thy love for all that thou shalt love without him, will not fill thee, but fly from thee.

397. The world contains nothing satisfying or lovely; but Jesus is unspeakable sweetness, and every

way desirable, who often visits His own by the consolation of inward peace.

398. Seek to become refreshed by the secret sweetness of Jesus, and in his pure intercourse to become possessed of the immeasurable depths of godliness; for He says, no one can come to the Father, but through me.

399. Without Jesus, all retirement is tumult; with Jesus everywhere it is tranquil and delightful. It is sweeter to be with Him on the cross, than without Him in heaven.

400. The time lasts not forever that Jesus withdrew Himself, for He must return again. But by this the faith of the lover becomes dearer than gold that is tried in the fire, and yet even then He is present to them, and certainly in a right, useful, and profitable way, although it happens difficult and disagreeable.

Ejaculation. Lord, I pray Thee accept still my service, for I am patient, desirous to accomplish my original sacrifice, and to aim forever to the honor and glory of Thy name. Let my heart never wander from Thy love, but let my soul and my love be right and constant in Thy service as long as I have breath within and am strong and able to remember Thee. May Thy praise from my mouth never cease, nor the abundance of Thy blessings be forgotten by my heart. If Thy servant should live many years, if even hundreds or thousands of years, may he never on that account become indolent or discouraged from serving Thee in humility and subjection, but may I in all things as devoutly and willingly serve Thee, as in that day when I called on Thee for the first time and decided to follow the Lord alone, with an entire and pure mind. Let not this purpose of mine be broken by any interrupting weakness or adversity. But as I now intend and now undertake what Thou, O God, hearest, I desire also to fulfill with Thy aid, what at any time my lips have said.

401. How lovely is he who takes delight in Jesus in prosperity or in adversity, and even gladly hungers and thirsts with Him, that he may eat and drink with Him hereafter. Thus love Him now, when He bestows good upon Thee; love Him when He takes away the same, and when besides He prepares affliction and calamities.

402. Let Jesus be thy only consolation wherever thou art, and as He dies for thee, thou shouldest thirst after His stay with thee.

403. Take care not to grieve the grace and mercy of Jesus, for when he is offended what peace canst thou have?

404. To everyone who devotes himself to external

vanities, devout communion with Christ becomes insipid.

105. What hast thou done, solitary, that thou hast forsaken the tumult of the world, and under the shadow of Christ, hast taken thy refuge, when in the meantime thou enjoyest quiet? How wisely hast thou chosen to be forgotten. How profitably mindest thou to live to God only, and to be seen in His eyes alone.

106. Provide a secret chamber in thine heart, which shall be the place thou wantest to accompany thy solitude.

107. For thy growth, it is not enough thou lovest retirement unless thou lovest holy retirement.

108. A salutary means against much conversation is to refrain from even necessary and lawful words, when no one commands. A burden is lighter and sweeter to bear, that one takes of free inclination and the instructions of the Holy Spirit.

109. Every word that is not serious or useful, should reasonably be far from pure minds.

110. The especially strong beginnings of any have often taken an especially remiss end, and some have again gone back. It is necessary to be earnest in the

beginning, but not without discretion.

Ejaculation. O thou highest good, thou true, eternal God, see, I take firm purpose of heart just to make a token of the union between me and thee. I will not love or regard any creature for the sake of thy noble, precious love; but I would despise all things and forsake myself as well as all things.

411. Some esteem it a thing of magnitude for any-one to maintain perpetual silence, which is indeed great; but to be silent and to talk as one should is greater. He who lives secluded and alone, can adopt silence as much as he chooses; but he who lives with the people, should live not only for himself, but be sociable with others.

412. He that is abroad and goes often with different men can hardly guard his mouth, that he shall not sometimes offend with a word, and O, that he may not destroy himself entirely. Therefore it is well, when it is permitted him of the Lord, to be in tranquillity and to continue himself therein; because things without and worldly can scarcely be handled without guilt and inward shame.

413. Let not a man accustom himself to superfluous things, unless he willingly refrains from many lawful things. For wise people want little, and when they satisfy themselves with necessaries they mind

not follies.

414. It is a sign we have little inward consolation, because so easy and so often we seek outward consolation. We are not therefore worthy to receive godly consolation, because we so gladly admit human and transitory.

415. It is no wonder that a pious soul depends entirely on Christ; he thinks it worthy of himself, not almost, but altogether to come to him.

416. Who would wish to go abroad when a beloved friend was come to him, without himself scarcely talking with him; much more would he go home, if he were abroad, and receive with attention so worthy a guest. So must all appear, who serve Christ, to regard Him for the future with esteem. O, sweetest friend, who, all-beloved, must be received with distinguished reverence.

417. Let this heart, which is hid with Christ, taste much of thy loveliness, though lusting after fleshly, temporal consolation; that is to say, "He shall never more thirst." It will be well with that one that has the house of his heart always prepared for the coming bridegroom and his sweetest friend.

418. Let Christ grant me only His society, and talk friendly with me, then shall I receive sweet consola-

tion enough.

419. When the mind is distracted with melancholy and disgust, then is everything troublesome to him to do, and because on all sides he sees himself entangled and comfortless; then is it suggested to him by the devil, that he should seek restoration in outward amusements. On this the pious Antonio has well said, "The only means to overcome the enemy, is the joy of the Spirit."

420. O, soldier of Christ, put on a manly heart, and be not so soon frightened by a rustling breeze. Obtain a new mind; stand firm against the manifold temptations of the devil; believe not his lies. The Lord is almighty; He will be Himself thy protector and thy exceeding great reward. He has power over thy passions, so that all this multitude shall be subdued to thy command.

Ejaculation. I love and praise Thee greatly, O Lord, that Thou hast condescended to call me through Thy grace giving me a good will and subduing me from the burden of sin. Thou hast brought me under Thy lovely yoke, and softened my heart by the salvation of Thy spirit, whom the world knows not, or sees, or feels. Prove this will, merciful Lord, and increase in me the gift of grace. As long as I shall be in Thy visible light, I would feel that Thy call to me is my greatest blessing.

421. Who, that was not worthy of contempt would before the presence of a king and his servants, pick up rottenness or grovel in the mud? And thou art (O shame!) the fool who hast begun this part. Then consider, in the presence of sacred Majesty and His holy angels, hast thou not been sinning?

422. Thou lettest thy heart wander about in the world. How canst thou rightly be called a spiritual man, who livest so far from God and thine own heart?

423. Whenever the course of thy life depends upon the mouth of men, thou shalt be at one time something, at another time nothing, but never free and peaceful. A righteous man lets not himself be deceived by sounding words, but gives attention to what pleases God.

424. Love the truth, not the conversation of men. In the hour of death, it shall be made manifest how deceptive are all the favors of the world, and how foolish will then appear the enjoyment we have sought in the praise of men.

425. He is thy friend, who pities thy sins and prays for thee; he rejoices in the increase of thy good and remembers thee with love. There is no truer friend than God, and He seeks but thy good.

426. What thou canst not improve, that bear with humility; be silent, turn to God, and pray rather. Then thou errest in much, when thou dost not always what thou promisest to another.

427. Cease to desire and thou wilt have no disappointments.

428. Nothing is permanent under the sun, all is subject to change. Nothing can be made sure but in God. The love of God is a safe foundation.

429. As long as the mind seeks consolation in earthly objects, it is always uneasy. In God is true joy of heart; without God, there is no peace or quietness.

430. Be more contented in torment and imprisonment with grace, than in a beautiful palace with a sinful conscience.

EJACULATION. O, my God, my love, in this place of pilgrimage, when shall I entirely be united to Thee, with all the strength of my soul, which Thou hast poured into me from Thee, freely and graciously. Let all Thy creatures be silent before Thee, O God. Talk thou only with me; be near me and illuminate me, Thou who art all in all and ever to be esteemed above all the glory of heaven.

431. Dost thou wish to be freed from sin and to be

made perfect in holiness, humble thyself before God, and before all creatures for the sake of God.

32. Humility gives peace, and harmony, and wisdom to endure all burdens and to man contempt of himself more profitable than the favor of vain praise.

33. He does what is truly great, who despises himself for the sake of God, and subdues himself in all things. He that is master of himself is lord of the whole world, and is an heir of heaven.

34. He that does not subdue himself in small things, how shall he master the greater? He that utterly forsakes himself, wishes for nought, but God.

35. To joy I have said, what hast thou to do with me without Jesus, who is my salvation? I desire not that thou shouldst come to me; let it be as Jesus has said. Pain should be more lovely to me than thou, for the sake of Jesus.

36. Have Jesus in thy heart and thou shalt be pure from all vileness.

37. He that engages little in foreign subjects, possesses much peace. That should be often said and again repeated, that it may be taken into consideration.

438. He produces much who desires much, but little who is satisfied with little; but no one will be perfectly filled, till he has enjoyed the highest good.

439. When thou art distracted by long conversation, collect thyself again by long silence; remain alone in retirement, and sighing over beginning sin. The heart is soon dissipated by things that one hears and sees, but frequent prayer shall drive out the noxious image and superfluous cares.

440. He who nor seeks or desires comfort on earth, and removes himself from all disquietings, can soon flee to Christ in heaven.

EJACULATION. I would love Thee, Lord, with my strength, purely, perfectly for Thy own sake, and all, also, which Thou hast created, for Thy sake; to love myself only for Thy sake, and Thee always more than myself; to love all things under Thee, and Thee alone above all good in heaven or earth. Thou alone art whole and perfect enough for me; therefore will desire nothing but Thee, who art before all and over all to be praised, O God, to all eternity. Amen.

441. Exalt not thyself before men on account of any goodness; within thou hast many wants that God knows, and that thou dost not see.

442. A humble man is insignificant in his own eyes,

who stands in the truth. Look justly and truly within; believe not lightly another's words.

443. In every good which thou dost say or think, depart not away from humility, lest thou lose all thou hast gained. No good deed profits which is not founded on humility, and directed by the honey of love flowing through, and filled with a pure contemplation of the honor of God.

444. Be guileless and without deceit, as a little child, pure from all sinfulness, so shalt thou be esteemed of God and man, and have peace in thyself.

445. What a freedom has the pure soul, that desires nothing of the state or pomp of the world, through love of the Lord Jesus Christ.

446. Blessed is he who employs all his time for the pleasure of God, and seeks not his own profit.

447. A good watcher of his heart examines carefully the door of his mouth, lest the holiness within should be lost by negligence of speech.

448. No time, no place, no work, no labor, no power should hinder us from prayer. God has His eyes upon us here and in all places. Canst thou not always pray with words, then shouldst thou be able, and ought to cry to God with the mind and the desire.

449. To be patient in bearing all grievances, to reject everything fleshly, to avoid everything worldly, is the way to heavenly life.

450. Bow humbly and willingly, O my soul, before God; mortify thyself before all creatures, for the sake of God. Think thyself in thy heart on the most trifling occasions.

EJACULATION. My God, when Thou enterest the house of the soul that loves Thee, thou wilt nourish him with milk, and Thou wilt sometimes carry him out of himself on account of the overflowing of Thy sweetness; therewith he may keep Thee without any bodily image. O truth! Truth, what can, what does not love accomplish? Then thou pressest upon him Thy heavenly word, and pointest out to him things new and old, and in Thy prosperous love and enjoyment, all human worlds come to an end. Consider my soul, dear Father, as that of a poor beggar, and with bowels of mercy, send the true bread from heaven, the good word full of grace and truth. Amen

451. Rejoice thyself, humble and silent brother, thou who art without falsehood or bitterness. Be obedient unto death. Despisest thou now thyself, and bearest thy cross after Christ, thou shalt enjoy thyself with all saints.

452. Sing and praise God, simply, brother, because

hou hast forsaken the wisdom of this world, and
he coils of the devil and his annual fair, and art far
removed from all care. Thank God.

53. Learn to yield thy own will and to overcome
he lust of the flesh. Stand fast and strive manfully
or the Lord thy God and His angels are with thee.

54. Hear, thou sighing turtle dove, thou who de-
irest to lead a solitary life, thou lover of everlasting
urity. When thou avoidest the bustle of the world,
o devote thyself to prayer and devout contempla-
ion, then thou approachest to the heavenly gates of
he angels.

55. No one lives so peacefully with others and no
ne goes so joyfully through the world, as one truly
bedient — the holy and humble heart, who denies
ntirely his own will.

56. Death is to me very necessary that I might de-
pise and subdue myself in all things for the sake of
hrist, who died and is arisen from the dead for me.

57. When I am destitute of all things and remain
lle, then I proceed heavenwards with Christ. Noth-
ig diverts me then, no consolation refreshes me,
xcept communion with Christ.

58. So much as I permit to happen for the sake of

Christ, so much I gain; so much as I depart from myself, so much I deviate. When I forsake myself, I find myself; when I seek myself, I lose myself.

459. I would remain with our beloved Lord, let Him go with me wherever He can.

460. What does it profit, that I put my hindrances upon another? Am I right, then it is good to be quiet and patient, it makes it no better to complain. Am I wrong, then it is better that I relax early than late.

EJACULATION. Lord God, be Thou blessed in all wherein Thou oppressest and burnest me. Let my afflictions be Thy praise and Thy glory. I must also glorify Thee upon the cross of my Lord Jesus Christ Let my pain be as great as Tis, and as long as please Thee. Fill me with Thy praise. I know Thou canst not do unrighteously; I pray that Thy will and highest pleasure may be perfected in me unto the end.

461. I must let all proceed along which is about me, and equally bear what is right and what is wrong; it is to me now often difficult, so I wish therein to yield, for soon all joy and complaining here will be ended.

462. Frequently am I deprived of all before I know and expect it; but therein must I learn to die also again to myself and to despise all inward

consolation and on the will of our Lord to lay my will.

163. I must expect the grace of God and shift and resign myself to poverty for I am not worthy of a farthing, but God is the beginning and end of all good.

164. All hindrances and confusion come from seeking self. Nature always seeks herself by various acts and devices, external and internal, small and great, and so is unwilling to be dead and despise herself. In this must they yet die and subject themselves. How otherwise shall the spirit console them, and they be united with Christ?

165. He that understands to keep himself poor and who can best suffer for the sake of God, and desires rather the less than the greater, he shall obtain the greatest peace and the highest joy with God.

166. One must look upon all things with a simple eye and a pure heart, and see that he regards nothing with sensual gratification, then shall all the things of this world; which may God, Himself, grant us.

167. One must prefer the will of God and the enjoyment of heaven to all the things of this world, which may God, Himself, grant us.

468. Pride is best overcome, when one is accustomed to occupy himself in despised business; diligently to suffer much wrong, and cheerfully to stay in the meanest place. To him, it is not difficult to be respectful; he is not far from true humility.

469. A sincere devout man loves solitude, that he may have a more free Sabbath with God.

470. Who trusts much to himself, places himself in peril. He acts very wisely, who subjects himself to one experienced. To desire the counsel and intercession of others is a sign of humility. God often says through another, what he manifests not openly to men by Himself.

EJACULATION. O Jesus, sweet name above all names, holy in heaven and upon earth, to Thee, at all times, in heaven upon earth and under the earth, both angels and men bow themselves. Thou art the way of righteousness, the excellence of the blessed, the hope of the needy, the salvation of the weak, the lover of the devout, and the consolation of all those who suffer affliction; be Thou to me a helper and guard in all difficulties, for the sake of thy holy name, which shall bless us in eternity. When I am poor, I will praise Thee; wherever I am, always will I praise Thee. Amen.

471. It is a praiseworthy thing, to be silent to an

injustice.

472. Learn to submit in all things, thus shalt thou obtain inward peace. I desire only that which I ought, and then shall I have heaven.

473. With patience and silence, the constant shall gain the greater peace. He is wise, who is really patient.

474. If I had this and if I had that, it would not be enough, "It satiates and displeases;" impress this on thy heart and nothing more shall harass thee.

475. One may see and enjoy all one wants, but it is all nothing if God is not there.

476. Why dost thou wish to complain and to run at one time here and another there? Wherever thou goest and comest, thou wilt not find all according to thy sense; everywhere appears something to be suffered. Canst thou not enjoy thyself, yet must thou suffer and agree to be satisfied always, overcoming all through patience. All will be as nothing, so long as thou dost not seek to please thyself in anything.

477. Think of thy going out of Egypt. Where is the spirit — the first zeal — the sure aim — the inflexible purpose — the love, strong as death?

478. Many say they would gladly be devout; they would gladly have virtue; they would have their lusts and passions subdued; but it is not enough that one wish, unless he lays his hand to the work. Thou must labor to inflict violence upon nature, as the Savior saith, "The kingdom of heaven suffereth violence, and violence taketh it by force, and know thou that the saints did not reach heaven by indolence and slumber?

479. The longer that thou procrastinatest, the worse wilt thou become; without labor and trouble thou canst not obtain the desired peace.

480. He that flies suffering, to him it will follow, tha this life shall be full of blemishes and deceit.

EJACULATION. Lord, cleanse my heart from all things of the creature and from all that can bind or eclipse me. Leave me simply fastened and attached purely and entirely to Thee. Give to me true, inward sacred peace, and to employ my mind tranquilly without any interruption.

481. Endure patiently, when thou wishest to please God and to watch unto good. Then all will reach thee for good, when thou receivest all misfortune as gain to the soul, from the hand of God. The straight way to heaven is to submit to the will of God.

482. The crime of another, throws a prejudice on no one; a weak word injures no one; if thou wilt only keep thyself unmoved and innocent. As a man is inwardly, so will the outward calamity affect him.

483. That is no great patience which lets one be tempted on a trifling occasion. Learn to be silent at the least thing that happens wrong; it becomes a rational man to lay his hand upon his mouth in an evil hour.

484. Shame on thee, that thou hast not learnt to bear with a little deficiency in thy brother. Thou art desirous that another should endure thy frailties; why showest thou not then the like mercy to another?

485. He is the most prudent, who bears his soul continually before him in his hands.

486. He does well who lets others pass on and roves, and judges, and regulates himself. The more one desires to look at others, the less can he look at himself. He who desires peace must dwell in Zion.

487. When one still so often finds himself stumbling, he must always anew lay hold on his heart and his hope.

488. How can one long be wrapped up in himself, who covets and desires many objects? He dissipates

himself to the four winds and lets himself be captured in the net of earthly lust.

489. He who desires all those things from himself, that each one besides lets stand as he found them, shall enjoy much peace.

490. He who desires to be a master in foreign things, it is no wonder if he is yet a scholar in his own.

Ejaculation. Grant, Lord, that in a sinful manner, I may not be inclined to anything external, nor wish to be known or regarded or loved of men, in a foolish way; for anything that one does out of Thee, in an inordinate manner, deceives and will deceive. Grant that I may draw no one —rough flattery or complaisancy; but put off all wisely from me, and conduct all safely to Thee; and that I may not regard or love anything, in any man or any creature, but what is Thine, and whereunto they were created.

491. This is thy work, to think alone upon thyself, and to put away from thee everything else, let it be what it may.

492. The way of the cross is our life. The way of election is to thee the littlest way, a bitter way, but a way of life and salvation; a short, straight, laborious but a perfect way.

193. Because the pure life of Christ was a cross, the life of a Christian must also be a cross.

194. The right cross and perhaps the greatest is to subdue one's own will.

195. The world honors the present, forgets the absent, and neglects the dying; therefore it is blessed to despise the deceived world and to follow truth.

196. The quantity of external business, is to the internal, a great hindrance, and a chilling of heavenly feelings.

197. As much as one is united with and illuminated by God, so much the more his mind is made tranquil and free from the cares of this world.

198. Guard much against such things as aim at worldly knowledge and human praise, but follow after the lowly things which Jesus has passed through.

199. The love of God shall not be proved by beautiful words, but through despising of thyself and all things transitory.

200. So long as thou art not truly humble and inwardly dead, it is not good for thee to investigate deep things. What does not make thee truly humble and acceptable to God, that desire not or regard.

501. Look upon the grace of God in others and love it, as just what it is, in truth, namely, the grace of God. It shall also become thine when thou lovest it as thine own; to every one that is humble, God again brings it.

CONCLUSION. The saints of God have written many and great things according as it was useful to men; yet never have they been able to speak as the Word itself does. Therefore we should not be satisfied with hearing outward discourses to entertain ourselves with the beauty of saying without, but always turn to that within and seek the Eternal which is above us, the one highest, eternal good.

SUMMARY. Sit down alone, my soul, and retire from all tumult and vice. Let nothing without affect thee; let nothing within interrupt thee. From love of the highest good, despise everything temporal. Turn entirely within; ascend a little upwards; rise above thyself; surmount all which is made for time; forsake all which is created; shut out all which exalts thee here, how high soever it may be, that thou mayst find the uncreated Word, that is exalted above all knowledge of the creature.

So much as thou studiest it, so much shall the Word come to thy help; so much as thou lookest into it, so much shall it illuminate thee; so much as thou art eager for it and lovest it, so much shall it inflame thee. Amen.

PRAYERS.

I.

Lord Jesus Christ, my hope, my only refuge, the consolation of my life, the former of my habits, this day I renounce all things in the world on account of my love to Thee and hope to continue in this to the honor of Thy name.

renounce all friends, parents, relations and neighbors, dear and known, and all my companions; all cities, towns, castles, villas, mountains and valleys, rivers and fountains, fields and meadows and groves; all magnificent and beautiful buildings, psalters, pipes, organs, music, songs, flowers, perfumes; all pleasures, society, feasts, conversations, visits, greetings, favors, honors, and delights of men; all scandal, rumors, plays, jokes, laughing, wandering, roamings, tumults, and idle occupations; all riches, property, offices, dignities, amusements, and recreations, and whatever can tempt, entice, and delight the flesh, or hinder or defile the soul.

Thee I choose this day to be my protector in God; the governor of my life; the provider for all my wants; the consolation of my griefs, troubles, and temptations, and all my labors: with whom to labor is necessary through all the days of my life, on account of Thy love and for the safety of my own soul. Thou art my refuge; Thou my home; Thou my city; Thou my habitation; Thou my food, my drink, my rest and my refreshment. Thou art my beloved companion, my intimate friend; Thou my nearest relation; Thou my brother and sister, and as my father and patron. Thou art the shepherd and keeper of my whole life, to whom I commend myself and all things confidently, for without Thee is no safety, not even life safe without Thee. Let, then, O God, Thy mercy be always over me; Thy grace always attend me. Let Thy eye be over me day and night; let Thy hand always protect me on the right hand and on the left, and wilt Thou think worthy to lead me to the dwelling place of Thy glory, by a right way, where I shall praise thee forever and ever. Amen.

II.

I pray Thee, Lord, my heavenly Father, who hast created all things by number, and weight, and measure, who lovest in Thy servants a cheerful service, direct all my actions according to Thy pleasure, and bring the opposing inclinations of my flesh under the government of the eternal appointment, and grant that I may entirely subdue my own will. Order all my inclinations so that in the outset I may reject the evil, and choose the good; love the pure, and learn to contemplate Thee without corporeal transformation.

Moderate my strength and labor, that I may not be entirely attached to earthly things, but always take care to subdue myself within.

Prove me so much in my longing for eternal things; in love of Thy heavenly virtue; in enjoyment of heavenly things, that, Lord God, I may obtain the greater honor, and the more salutary progress.

Grant me that out of Thy gracious visitings, there commence no obstinacy of highmindedness, and that the plague of vain honors may not torment me. Let me not be deceived by Satan, nor be led away by false affections. May I not by any flightiness of piety, deviate from the community of thy children. May I not be injured by immoderate bodily exercise.

Grant that I may do everything with discretion, and with great reverence for Thy majesty; purely and freely worship Thee. May I walk in thy sight without confusion of mind, or love of terrestrial objects.

Grant that I, O God, may possess a humble, peaceable mind and never forsake Thee, distracted by earth, nor be attached to any creature with sinful inclinations, but give up my heart, pure and peaceful, to Thee; that I may always look to heaven with humility, and upon Thee, my God, may I bestow my secret remembrances; that I may not be tempted with visible objects, but continue a despiser of the world.

Grant that I may perform outward actions according to the circumstances of place and the convenience of time; that I may bring no shame to myself within; but let all labor and business be undertaken for Thy sake. Give me Thine aid, that I may be the freer to serve Thee.

Grant also, that all which I do externally, or which I perceive within, with a simple and pure heart, may be accomplished to the greater honor of Thy name, and for the love of Thy will become so much the more pleasant; and may I give myself to Thee willingly, as well in everything which is acceptable to Thee, as in those things which are against nature.

Give to me to bear patiently the burden of this pleasant life till Thou call me, and may I faithfully commend to Thee, my Creator, my body and soul. Remember me, O Lord, till the time of my last hour, and deal graciously with Thy servant, who confides not in his own goodness, but in Thy mercy and goodness. Amen.

III.

Beloved and Holy Lord God, my Father, I am not worthy to be comforted or visited by Thee, but to be punished and scourged with hard blows.

I deserve many penalties, and various tribulations,

or I have greatly sinned, and been ungrateful to thy innumerable kindnesses. I am not as worthy or as faithful in other goods, like my devout brethren, to be reckoned among thy heavenly guests, and to partake of Thy consolations.

But I beseech Thee, heavenly Father, dear and holy Lord, make me to kiss. They have many and great consolations, whom Thou lovest with especial favor; to me, the least and most miserable, it would be well and acceptable that Thou wouldest not share in afflicting me with trouble and adversity.

Give me patience, holy Lord, and let all tribulation and affliction be desirable and pleasant above all other consolation. And this, especially, I will suffer for Thine honor, and be grateful, not for increasing my gain, or hoping either for reward. Let me gain nothing more, than cheerfully to suffer for Thine honor, and even to the last, to desire to be despised and counted as nothing, and before all men, may I be truly humble and subdued.

Pour into my heart, O my God, the highest truth — eternal light — that I may be vile and despise myself, and live in this world as a pilgrim, a poor unknown, a neglected solitary, forsaken of all creatures, and unworthy of human consolation, and that besides in Thee, I may seek consolation nowhere else.

Let me be as one dead upon the earth, think myself as one buried in the world, whose memory no longer exists, and of whose life nothing remains, except a low sepulchre under ground. O Thou eternal wisdom of the Father, grant that I may think of these things with an earnest mind.

O, gracious, kind Jehovah, be merciful to me, an unworthy and great sinner; Thou who came into the world for the sake of sinners, and was crucified for their expiation and was condemned to a painful death, Thou hast not withdrawn thyself.

The End

THE LITTLE ALPHABET IN THE SCHOOL OF CHRIST.

by

Thomas A Kempis

Edited by Mel Waller

St Athanasius Press

All Rights Reserved 2014

The pupil: Lord, show me your way and teach me your paths I entreat you, O my God, direct me in the way of a pious life, for the salvation of my soul. Teach me the measure of your commandments, so that I may understand them. Remove from me my blindness, that I may perceive what you require. Pour out upon me the grace of your Spirit, to conduct me in straight paths. God, the school master: I will give you understanding and show you the way. I will guide you with my eyes.

LESSON 1. Ama Nesciri.

Love to be unknown, and to be esteemed as nothing. This will be more salutary and useful than to be praised of men.

LESSON II. Bonevolus Esto.

Be benevolent to all, good or bad, and troublesome to no one.

LESSON III. Custodi Cor.

Keep your heart from wandering, your tongue from idle conversation, and your other senses under severe discipline.

LESSON IV. Dilige Solitudinem.

Love solitude and silence, and you will find great quiet, and a good conscience; but in the midst of the crowd, there is often a bustle and much distraction of heart.

LESSON V. Elige paupertatem.

Prefer poverty and simplicity; then you will be content with a little, and not so easily complain.

LESSON VI. Fuse homines.

Shun society, and the tumult of the world (as much as you can), for you can not devote yourself to God and man, to things eternal and temporal.

LESSON VII. Gratias age.

Thank God always with heart and tongue, whatever happens to you, either of afflictions or sorrows. God dispenses all things wisely in the world by a just and determined decree from all eternity.

LESSON VIII. Humilia te.

Humble yourself in all things, and before all persons, and you will obtain favor from all. You will be both accepted of God and beloved by men; and the devil will flee the quicker from you on account of the virtue of humility, so widely different from himself.

LESSON IX. Intentio pura.

In every good work possess a pure intention; thus will you please God, who looks upon the heart, and loves the just and upright.

LESSON X. Carissimi qui premunt.

Consider as friends and supporters, the most precious those who persecute and revile you. For if you art truly wise and take heed, you wilt reap an advantage. They shall profit you for good who oppose you for evil.

LESSON XI. Lahore et dolore.

The kingdom of God is obtained by labor and sorrow, with groaning and lamentation; in pleasures and honors, heaven is lost.

LESSON XII. Magnus qui minimus.

It is a great gift of God to be poor in this world for Christ, and to hold the lowest seat. Swelling pride seeks the highest seat. The devil always entices to the highest seats, to pursue honors, to fly contempt; thus exalting himself he falls back, since after brief authority he becomes poor. Esteem the smallest favors bounteous, and you will be worthy to receive the greatest.

LESSON XIII. Neminem sperne.

Despise no one; injure no one; console the afflicted; succor the destitute; but never praise yourself.

LESSON XIV. Omne tempus Deo.

You may profitably devote your whole time to God, for nothing is more precious than the time in which you are able to obtain forever the kingdom of God. You may be amiable, courteous, affable to all, without dissipation. Give glory of all blessings to God. Do nothing without reflection and deliberation.

LESSON XV. Placet-ne Deo.

In every undertaking, first inquire, will it please God, or displease him? Act not against your conscience, from fear o affection. In doubt, recur to the gospel of Christ. Trust not too much to yourself, learn rather to be silent than to speak, — it is safer to be in the shade than to shine.

LESSON XVI. Quid ad te.

You should not judge, or interest yourself in relation to others in what does not concern you, that you may always have peace. He who imitates the world and lives singly, will be more loved and will more quickly attain to a happy end. He who performs punctually his duty, will be happier afterwards.

LESSON XVII. Reverte.

Return to the bottom of your heart, and shut the doors of your mouth, lest you begin to stray on account of the fascinations of the world, to the counsels of the devil. Evil speeches injure, gaieties tempt, accusations disturb. Depart, therefore, from an ill tempered ignorant dissipated man, and continue with God in silence.

LESSON XVIII. Sobrius esto.

Be temperate in food, modest in apparel, careful in speech, civil in manners, prudent in counsel, strong in adversity, humble in prosperity, grateful for favors, cheerful under contempt, patient in affliction, discreet in all your actions.

LESSON XIX. Time Deum.

Fear God, that you may not offend by negligence or deficiency. Refrain from presumption in prosperity, and despair in adversity. The fear of God causes to shun sin, solicits to good works. Trust all to God, and what is oppressive to you, he will quickly make easy; he will be your peace in much suffering, all tribulation is light for eternal life.

LESSON XX. Vende omnia.

Sell all your possessions to God, and he will give richer comforts to you, a present favor in one hour. No one is richer and none more liberal to him, who gives himself and all things to God, who buys Christ by loving him who redeemed the world by the cross.

LESSON XXI. Christus sit vita.

Let Christ be your life, your reading, your meditation, your conversation. He your desire, your gain, all your hope and your reward. If you seek any other than God, you will suffer loss; you shall labor and not find rest.

LESSON XXII. Hymnos cane Deo.

To sing hymns and psalms to God, is the duty of the spiritual and solitary with whom angelic choirs rejoice, praising God continually in the kingdom of heaven. To serve the flesh is the death of the soul, food of worms, nest of demons, life of sheep, fuel of diseases, corruption of bodies, pollution of manners, loss of good things, and acquisition of many evils and sorrows. To serve God, happiness of soul, health of body, prudence of mind and life. He sings sweet hymns to God, who praises him continually in the midst of tribulation. The beginning and end of religious enjoyment is to love God in heart and to praise him with the mouth, and to strengthen his brother by example.

LESSON XXIII Zacchee descende.
Brother Zaceheus do come down from that eminence of secular knowledge, come and learn in the school of God the way of humility, gentleness and patience; by which you can, Christ teaching you, obtain hereafter the glory of eternal happiness. Amen.

CONCLUSION.

Write, young novice, that alphabet on your heart, as for the book of life. Through every day read the little chart, to accustom yourself to good manners. There are few words, but they contain great mysteries, and a work of perfection. They adorn the external, and give peace within. With self-contempt and self-loathing, begins the life of a good religious Christian, and he goes forward in the contemplation of God.

BENEDICTION.

Happy is that disciple, who follows Christ over rough ways, giving up to him all his wishes and opposition, bearing his cross daily for Christ; that he may enjoy with him great glory and eternal life. Amen.

Other Titles Available from
St Athanasius Press
www.stathanasiuspress.com

Be sure to check our website for the newest titles
being offered and for our latest contact information!

A Commonitory for the Antiquity and Universality
of the Catholic Faith Against the
Profane Novelties of all Heresies
by Vincent of Lerins

A Golden Book of Three Tabernacles:
Poverty, Humility and Patience
by Thomas A Kempis

A Little Book of Eternal Wisdom
by Blessed Henry Suso

A Short Catechism of Cardinal Bellarmine
by Cardinal Robert Bellarmine

A Thought from St Ignatius Loyola
for Each Day of the Year
by St Ignatius Loyola

A Thought From Thomas A Kempis
for Each Day of the Year
by Thomas A Kempis

A Treatise of Discretion
by St Catherine of Siena

A Treatise of Divine Providence
& A Treatise of Obedience
by St Catherine of Siena

A Treatise of Prayer
by St Catherine of Siena

A Treatise on the Particular Examen of Conscious
by Fr Luis De La Palma, SJ

Catholic An Essential and Exclusive Attribute
of the True Church
by Rt Rev Msgr Capel

Christ Our Rest and King
by Henry Edward Manning

Cochems Explanation of the Holy Sacrifice of the
Mass
by Fr Martin Cochem

Collection of Catholic Prayers and Devotions

Collection of Thomas A Kempis Classics
by Thomas A Kempis

Devotion to the Nine Choirs of Angels
by Henri Marie Boudon

Devotion to the Sacred Heart of Jesus
by Fr John Croiset, SJ

Dignity and Duties of the Priest or Selva
by St Alphonsus M Liguori, CSSR

Explanation of the Psalms & Canticles
in the Divine Office
by St Alphonsus M Liguori, CSSR

For Passion Sunday
by Thomas A Kempis

Humility of Heart
by Fr Cajetan Mary da Bergamo

Indifferentism or
Is One Religion as Good as Another?
by John Maclaughlin

Life of St Leonard of Port Maurice
by Fr Dominic Devas, OFM

Modernism
by Cardinal Mercier

On Cleaving to God English/Latin
by St Albert the Great

On Contempt for the World or
De Contemptu Mundi
by St Eucherius of Lyon

On Divine Love and the Means of Acquiring It
by St Alphonsus M Liguori, CSSR

Preparation for Death
by St Alphonsus M Liguori, CSSR

Religious Orders of Women
in the United States (1930 Photos included)
by Elinor Tong Dehey

Saint Athanasius:
The Father of Orthodoxy
by F. A. Forbes

Sermons for All the Sundays in the Year
by St Alphonsus M Liguori, CSSR

Sermons Upon Various Subjects
by St Alphonsus M Liguori, CSSR

St Alphonsus Liguori on the Council of Trent
by St Alphonsus M Liguori, CSSR

St Charity: A True Life Catholic Pro Life Story
by Mel Waller

Ten Reasons Proposed to His Adversaries
for Disputation in the Name of the Faith
by St Edmund Campion

The Art of Dying Well
by St Robert Bellarmine

The Cross and the Shamrock
by Hugh Quigley

The Cure of Ars
by Kathleen O'Meara

The Dialogue of the Seraphic Virgin
St Catherine of Siena
by St Catherine of Siena

The Douay Catechism of 1649
by Henry Tuberville, D.D.

The Eternal Happiness of the Saints
by St Robert Bellarmine

The History of Heresies
by St Alphonsus M Liguori, CSSR

The Holy Eucharist
by St Alphonsus M Liguori, CSSR

The Holy Ways of the Cross
by Henri Marie Boudon

The Life of St Dominic Savio
by St John Bosco

The Little Kempis
or Short Sayings and Prayers
by Thomas A Kempis

The Love of Souls Or
Reflections and Affections
on the Passion of Jesus Christ
by St Alphonsus M Liguori, CSSR

The Maxims and Sayings of St Philip Neri
by St Philip Neri

The Mind's Road to God
by St Bonaventure

3 Volume Set
The Practice of Christian and Religious Perfection
by Fr Alphonsus Rodriguez, SJ

The Practice of the Love of Jesus Christ
by St Alphonsus M Liguori, CSSR

The Raccolta or A Manual of Indulgences
1957 Edition

The Roman Index of Forbidden Books
by Francis S Betten, SJ

The Spiritual Conflict and Conquest
by Dom J Castaniza, OSB

The Treatise on Purgatory
by St Catherine of Genoa

The Triumph of the Cross
by Fra Girolamo Savonarola

The Valley of Lilies & The Little Garden of Roses
by Thomas A Kempis

The Way of Salvation and Perfection
by St Alphonsus M Liguori, CSSR

Treatise on Prayer
by St Alphonsus M Liguori, CSSR

Vera Sapentia or True Wisdom
Thomas A Kempis

Visits to the Most Holy Sacrament
and the Blessed Virgin Mary
by St Alphonsus M Liguori, CSSR

Vocations Explained
by A Vincentian Father

Where We Got the Bible
by Henry G Graham

New Titles are Being Added Often!

Printed in the USA
CPSIA information can be obtained
at www.ICGtesting.com
LVHW042247120524
780094LV00027B/218